Wor

for

The Myth of Normal

Trauma, Illness & Healing in a Toxic Culture

Ingenious Reads

Legal & Disclaimer

The information contained in this book and its contents is not designed to replace or take the place of any form of medical or professional advice; and is not meant to replace the need for independent medical, financial, legal, or other professional advice or services, as may be required. The content and information in this book have been provided for educational and entertainment purposes only.

The content and information contained in this book have been compiled from sources deemed reliable, and it is accurate to the best of the Author's knowledge, information, and belief. However, the Author cannot guarantee its accuracy and validity and cannot be held liable for any errors and/or omissions. Further, changes are periodically made to this book as and when needed. Where appropriate and/or necessary, you must consult a professional (including but not limited to your doctor, attorney, financial advisor, or such other professional advisor) before using any of the suggested remedies, techniques, or information in this book.

Upon using the contents and information contained in this book, you agree to hold harmless the Author from and against any damages, costs, and expenses, including any legal fees potentially resulting from the application of any of the information provided by this book. This disclaimer applies to any loss, damages, or injury caused by the use and application, whether directly or

2

Download Your Free Gift

Before you go any further, why not pick up a free gift from me to you?

Smarter Brain – a 10-part video training series to help you develop higher IQ, memory, and creativity – FAST!

www.Geniusreads.com

Introduction

The book *The Myth of Normal* by Gabor Maté and Daniel Maté is a guide to discovering how our emotional well-being and social connectivity are deeply integrated with health, disease, and addictions.

This book is a powerful and in-depth combination of science and stories that helps us see how stress shapes our well-being. It urges us to question our assumptions about who we are and investigate deeply into who we may become.

On a societal level, this book makes us question our entire social construct. We find the courage to look at its flaws and toxicities on all levels.

Gabor talks about the contradiction between how the world as a whole has never been as obsessed with health and fitness as it is now and the rampant diagnoses of mental health issues, especially among the young. He brings to us a revolutionary approach to everything health related – that illness is not bad luck; it is "an expected and therefore normal consequence of abnormal, unnatural circumstances".

We achieve a lot from reading this book, primarily coming to the understanding that our emotions, culture, and bodies, are not separate. Wellness comes from integration.

The book is divided into 5 parts:

- Part 1: Our Interconnected Nature (Chapters 1 to 7)
- Part 2: The Distortion of Human Development (Chapters 8 to 14)

- Part 3: Rethinking Abnormal: Afflictions as Adaptations (Chapters 15 to 18)
- Part 4: The Toxicities of our Culture (Chapters 19 to 24)
- Part 5: Pathways to Wholeness (Chapters 25 to 33)

We find both refuge and solace in this book. It is a compass for times that are disorienting. We learn that our trauma is not personal but collective. It comes from a society that undermines our need for authenticity, connection, and meaning. The authors not only tell us what is wrong, but they also guide us on how to make it right.

Once we can see clearly how things are, the process of healing, essentially returning to wholeness, can begin.

Authors' Introduction

Gabor Maté is a physician, renowned speaker, and bestselling author. He is highly sought after for his expertise in childhood development, trauma, addictions, and the relationship between stress and illness.

Gabor is known for co-developing a psychotherapeutic method known as *Compassionate Inquiry*. It helps unveil that which lies beneath the appearance we show to the outside world. In his bestselling book *In the Realm of Hungry Ghosts: Close Encounters with Addiction*, Gabor looks intimately at this widespread human affliction of addiction.

He has been awarded the Order of Canada and the Civil Merit Award of the City of Vancouver for his extensive and groundbreaking medical work and writing.

Daniel Maté is a composer, lyricist, and playwright. His work has been honored with the Edward Kleban Prize, a Jonathan Larson Foundation Grant, and the Cole Porter Award for Music and Lyrics.

He runs a 'mental chiropractic' service called *Take a Walk with Daniel*. He is the host of a YouTube series called *Lyrics to Go*. He also co-leads the popular workshop *Hello Again: A Fresh Start for Parents and their Adult Children* with his father Gabor Maté.

Chapter 1: The Last Place You Want to Be: Facets of Trauma

This first chapter of *The Myth of Normal* by Gabor Maté and Daniel Maté begins with a story of how Gabor when he received a text from his wife that she would not be able to come to pick him up from the airport, sulked for the next 24 hours. He says his response was not so much to the present moment as it was from an imprint of trauma from the distant past.

Trauma, when translated from its Greek origin, means wound. Gabor says that it is our woundedness and how we deal with that that determines much of our behavior, social habits, and thinking about the world. It also determines our capability or incapability for rational thought even in the areas of the greatest importance to our lives. It often shows up in our closest partnerships.

Peter Levine, the leading trauma psychologist and healer of the present century, calls certain shocks that alter our biological, psychological, and social equilibrium to such an extent that their memory dominates and taints all other experiences as "the tyranny of the past".

One such behavior is 'detachment'. It was seen that children who were separated from their mothers for days or weeks, showed a certain degree of detachment when they were reunited. It was the child's way of expressing that since the mother abandoned them, they would not reconnect with them. It was a way to protect themselves from the pain of future abandonment. This behavior shows up throughout our lifetimes, whenever we are faced with an incident that even vaguely resembles the original imprint.

Psychiatrist Bessel van der Kolk has written that all trauma is "preverbal". Levine explains this by saying that conscious memory is only the tip of a very deep iceberg. Our experiences can be much more deeply ingrained than that.

Trauma is often understood as something that is abnormal, unusual, and exceptional. However, if there was someone untouched by trauma, that person would be an outlier.

Gabor describes trauma as "an inner injury". He says it is "not what happens to you but what happens inside you". It is a psychic injury that gets lodged in our nervous system, mind, and body that lasts long past the originating event, and is triggerable at any moment. Trauma keeps us stuck in the past, limits who we can be, diminishes our sense of worth, hampers relationships, and contributes to illnesses of all kinds.

There are two kinds of trauma:

1. **Capital-t Trauma:** It is what underlies much of what gets labeled as mental illness. It can also cause physical illness by driving inflammation, elevating physiological stress, and impairing the healthy functioning of genes. It occurs when things happen that should not have happened, for example, child abuse, violence, or the loss of a parent.

2. **Small-t Trauma:** These are the less memorable but hurtful misfortunes of childhood. They could have occurred because of childhood bullying, harsh comments of an otherwise well-meaning parent, or a lack of sufficient emotional connection with a nurturing adult. It can lead to disconnection from the self.

The fracturing of the self is the essence of trauma. Levine writes that trauma is a loss of connection to ourselves, our families, and the world around us.

Gabor says that an event is traumatizing or retraumatizing only if it diminishes oneself, which means it leaves one psychically or physically more limited in a persistent way.

Being disconnected from one's body is prominent in the life experience of those who have gone through trauma and is an essential aspect of trauma. The suppression of the bodily response in the wake of childhood trauma is akin to the *freeze* response, which occurs when fight or flight are both impossible. A traumatized nervous system does not get to unfreeze.

Trauma robs us of our capacity for response flexibility – our capacity to pause between a stimulus and response and use that pause to choose a response we tilt more towards. The earlier and more severe the trauma, the less time the brain has to develop response flexibility. It leads to becoming stuck in predictable and automatic defensive reactions, especially to stressful stimuli. Also, the more severe the trauma, the more the loss of compassion for oneself.

If we can look at trauma as something that occurred inside us as a result of what happened outside us, then healing and reconnection become possible. When we face it without denial or overidentification, we open a door to health and balance.

Goal:

This chapter of *The Myth of Normal* begins with a definition of the word 'trauma'. It tells us what trauma is and what it does. We learn about the two types of trauma – capital-t and small-t. We then understand what trauma is not. Gabor talks about how trauma separates us from our bodies and creates disconnection, how it splits us from our gut feelings, how it limits our response flexibility, how it fosters a shame-based view of the self and distorts our view of the world, and how it alienates us from the present.

Lesson:

Activity 1:
Ask yourself the following questions in your assessment of having experienced trauma:
a) Where do you fit on the broad trauma spectrum?

b) Which marks of trauma do you think you could have carried all or most of your life?

c) What have the impacts of these marks of trauma been?

d) What possibilities could open up for you were you to become more familiar, even intimate, with your experiences of trauma?

Checklist:

Key learnings from this chapter are:
- [ ] Trauma, when translated from its Greek origin, means wound. It is our woundedness and how we deal with it that determines much of our behavior, social habits, and thinking about the world.
- [ ] Peter Levine calls shocks that alter our biological, psychological, and social equilibrium to an extent that their memory dominates and taints all other experiences as "the tyranny of the past".
- [ ] Psychiatrist Bessel van der Kolk has written that all trauma is "preverbal".
- [ ] Trauma is often understood as something that is abnormal, unusual, and exceptional. However, if there was someone untouched by trauma, that person would be an outlier.
- [ ] Gabor describes trauma as "an inner injury". He says it is "not what happens to you but what happens inside you".
- [ ] Gabor says that an event is traumatizing or retraumatizing only if it diminishes oneself, which means it leaves one psychically or physically more limited in a persistent way.
- [ ] Being disconnected from one's body is prominent in the life experience of those who have gone through trauma and is an essential aspect of trauma.
- [ ] Trauma robs us of our capacity for response flexibility – our capacity to pause between a stimulus and response and use that pause to choose a response we tilt more towards.

Action Plan:

☐ You can use this process of elimination checklist to assess if something can be classified as trauma:
- It does not limit you, constrict you, diminish your capacity to feel or think or to trust or assert yourself, to experience suffering without giving in to despair or to witness it with compassion. ☐
- It does not keep you from holding your pain, sorrow, and fear without being overwhelmed and without having to escape habitually into work, compulsive self-soothing, or compulsive self-stimulating by whatever means.
☐
- You are not left compelled either to aggrandize or efface yourself for the sake of gaining acceptance or to justify your existence.
☐
- It does not impair your capacity to experience gratitude for the beauty and wonder of life.
☐

Chapter 2: Living in an Immaterial World: Emotions, Health, and the Body-Mind Unity

The second chapter of *The Myth of Normal* by Gabor Maté and Daniel Maté shares a story of a woman named Caroline who was battling cancer. Against all medical statistics, she lived on for two decades longer than her physician's prognosis.

Through her story, we learn about the term 'superautonomous self-sufficiency' – an exaggerated and outsize aversion to asking anything of anyone. It is a form of suppression that develops as a coping reaction to developmental trauma.

Traditional healing practices have understood and worked with the intricate and inseparable connection between the mind and the body. Most of us know this is true at a gut level. Body and mind cannot be understood separately from each other.

It has been seen in research that extreme suppression of anger and other emotions was significantly higher in those with cancer. A paper on Amyotrophic lateral sclerosis (ALS) found that the staff could predict who would be diagnosed with the condition by assessing the patient's niceness. Too nice meant they would surely be diagnosed.

Similarly, anger and grief also have powerful physiological dimensions. Higher levels of PTSD symptoms have been associated with increased risks of ovarian cancer. There is striking evidence to prove that emotional stress is inseparable from our physical state.

Psychoneuroimmunology is a relatively new science that maps the many links of bodymind unity. It includes the connections between our emotions and our nervous and immune systems. It also studies how stress might instigate disease. It is built on the premise of unity between mind, brain, nervous and immune systems, and the hormonal system. Its core lesson is that what our bodies experience from conception onwards affects how we think, feel, perceive, and behave.

Stress is a mandatory survival function. It can show up either as an immediate reaction or as a prolonged state. By reducing stress wherever possible and attending to our emotions, we can greatly reduce its effects on physical health.

Goal:

The second chapter of *The Myth of Normal* shares research about the intricate and inseparable connection between mind and body. We learn about various studies that show how certain emotions are linked to certain illnesses. We understand the machinery of stress and how it impacts our physical health.

Lesson:

Activity 1:
Think about your childhood. Write down any 5 events or situations that you think could have shaped your behaviors and attitudes.

1.

2.

3.

4.

5.

Checklist:
Key learnings from this chapter are: ☐ 'Superautonomous self-sufficiency' is an exaggerated and outsize aversion to asking anything of anyone. It is a form of suppression that develops as a coping reaction to developmental trauma. ☐ Body and mind cannot be understood separately from each other. ☐ There is striking evidence to prove that emotional stress is inseparable from our physical state. ☐ Psychoneuroimmunology maps the many links of bodymind unity. It includes the connections between our emotions and our nervous and immune systems. It also studies how stress might instigate disease. ☐ By reducing stress wherever possible and attending to our emotions, we can greatly reduce its effects on physical health.

Action Plan:
☐ We learn about the suppression of emotions and its impact on physical health. Create a journal and write down any situations from the day where you think you would have suppressed how you were feeling.

Are you enjoying the book so far?

If so, please help me reach more readers by taking 30 seconds to write just a few words on Amazon

Or, you can choose to leave one later...

Chapter 3: You Rattle My Brain: Our Highly Interpersonal Biology

In the third chapter of *The Myth of Normal* by Gabor Maté and Daniel Maté, we explore the connection between ourselves and the world – from people to the rocks, the sky, and all creatures. We exist in relationship to all and are affected by all.

We understand how different spiritual texts, poets, and philosophers talk about our interconnected threads. Our personal uniqueness or our ego refers to a separate self but we barely exist as individuals. Our biology – mental, emotional, social, and natural environments – is also interpersonal.

Dr. Daniel Siegel introduced the term interpersonal neurobiology. His team found that our brains and minds do not function in isolation from other brains and minds. Nothing about us, mental or physical, can be comprehended outside of the larger context in which we exist.

The closer we are to someone, the more our physiology interacts with theirs. Children's physiology is particularly affected by the emotional states of their caregivers. Their stress hormone levels and diseases like asthma are affected by the atmosphere at home and the emotions of one or both parents. Racism is another risk factor.

Interpersonal biology explains why loneliness is a killer, especially in older people who are separated from social connections, support, and pleasures. The negative effects of deficient interpersonal relationships are comparable to such risk factors like smoking and alcohol. They exceed the dangers posed by lack of physical activity and obesity.

Goal:

The third chapter of *The Myth of Normal* explores our interconnectedness with everything around us. We understand how different spiritual texts, poets, and philosophers talk about our interconnected threads. We also learn about interpersonal neurobiology.

Lesson:

Activity 1:
This chapter educates us about interconnectedness. Think about all the ways in which our lives are connected to everyone else in the world. Some of the ways to do this are:
- What did you have for breakfast? Where did it come from?

- When you take a shower, think about who makes it possible for you to have access to clean water every day.

- Think about the house you live in and the different things it is made of.

Checklist:

Key learnings from this chapter are:
- [ ] We exist in relationship to all and are affected by all.
- [ ] Our personal uniqueness or our ego refers to a separate self but we barely exist as individuals.
- [ ] Our biology – mental, emotional, social, and natural environments – is also interpersonal.
- [ ] Dr. Daniel Siegel introduced the term interpersonal

neurobiology. His team found that our brains and minds do not function in isolation from other brains and minds.
- The closer we are to someone, the more our physiology interacts with theirs.
- Children's physiology is particularly affected by the emotional states of their caregivers.
- Interpersonal biology explains why loneliness is a killer, especially in older people who are separated from social connections, support, and pleasures.

Action Plan:

- We learn about how we are affected by the people we are close to and interact with. Think about 3 day to day events where the reactions or behavior of someone affected your mood:

1.

2.

3.

Chapter 4: Everything I'm Surrounded By: Dispatches from the New Science

The fourth chapter of *The Myth of Normal* by Gabor Matéé and Daniel Maté starts with a discussion on telomeres – minuscule DNA structures at the end of chromosomes. Telomeres also have social implications in that they bear the markers of the circumstances in which we live our lives.

Neuroscientist Candace Lewis, in her work, talks about her findings which show how malleable we are as an organism and how responsive we stay to environmental cues throughout our lives.

Our culture places great emphasis on our genetic inheritance. It is believed to determine who we are, what we suffer from, and what we are capable of. We now know that genes are not life's language. Genes are building blocks. But it is through the workings of epigenetics that they are activated or quieted. Therefore, our experiences determine how our genetic potential expresses itself.

Genes respond to their environment. They cannot function without environmental signals. Circumstances can shape how genes adjust to their environment.

Studies on rats have shown how the quality of early maternal care impacts the offspring's brain's capacity to respond to stress in a healthy way into adulthood. The quality of maternal care also affects the receptor activity for estrogen – a key female hormone. These effects were more epigenetic rather than genetic. Even rat fathers transmitted the disturbing effects of their stress through their sperm.

The epigenome also gets affected by socioeconomic circumstances. Those who were born well-off showed different gene expression compared to those who grew up disadvantaged. Racism and discrimination have been seen as creating a difference in gene activity that increases inflammation.

At birth, telomeres have many units. As we age, these go on becoming fewer. They are a measure of our biological clock rather than our chronological age. The amount of stress, adversity, or trauma we endure determines our biological age. Stress shortens telomeres and ages our chromosomes.

Conversely, experiences that build stress resilience can lengthen our telomeres, even when we are faced with an adversity or illness.

Goal:

The fourth chapter of *The Myth of Normal* educates us on telomeres – minuscule DNA structures at the end of chromosomes. Telomeres also have social implications in that they bear the markers of the circumstances in which we live our lives. We learn about how malleable we are as an organism and how responsive we stay to environmental cues throughout our lives.

Lesson:

Activity 1:
We learned about how stress affects our biological age. Can you think of 3 areas of your everyday life where you can reduce your stress, perhaps by giving up on a habit or changing a response:
1.

2.

3.

Checklist:

Key learnings from this chapter are:
- [ ] Telomeres have social implications in that they bear the markers of the circumstances in which we live our lives.
- [ ] Genes are not life's language. Genes are building blocks. It is through the workings of epigenetics that they are activated or quieted.
- [ ] Our experiences determine how our genetic potential expresses itself.

- The epigenome also gets affected by socioeconomic circumstances. Those who were born well-off showed different gene expression compared to those who grew up disadvantaged.
- Racism and discrimination have been seen as creating a difference in gene activity that increases inflammation.
- The amount of stress, adversity, or trauma we endure determines our biological age.
- Experiences that build stress resilience can lengthen our telomeres, even when we are faced with an adversity or illness.

Action Plan:

- A simple way to reduce stress: Cultivate a daily mindfulness practice. You can try breathing practices, sitting still with yourself, observing the body and mind, observing your feelings and thoughts, mindful walking, and mindful eating. Over time, you will be able to become more observant of what is happening inside and feel less of an urge to hide those feelings with unhelpful behaviors or substances.

Chapter 5: Mutiny on the Body: The Mystery of the Rebellious Immune System

The fifth chapter of *The Myth of Normal* by Gabor Maté and Daniel Maté begins with a discussion on autoimmune conditions. Autoimmunity is the immune system's assault on the body it is supposed to defend. 80 or more conditions have been so far dubbed as autoimmune.

Autoimmune conditions are characterized by inflammation of the afflicted organs, tissues, and body parts. Medicines are usually prescribed to suppress the body's immune activity. However, autoimmune diseases can be hard for physicians to pinpoint at first. They are among the great unsolved mysteries of western medicine. They are considered to be "idiopathic" in nature, which means of unknown origin.

Since the cause of autoimmune diseases has not been identified yet, it has not been possible for medicine to cure or reverse them. People are therefore consigned to prolonged deterioration.

The first mystery around them is around why they are becoming more frequent. The second is their highly skewed gender distribution. Women are much more likely to develop autoimmune conditions compared to men.

The term "neurogenic inflammation" refers to stress-induced inflammation that gets triggered by discharges of the nervous system. Research has shown that early adversity can lead to inflammation in adult life. Our personality traits reflect how as children we learned to accommodate our emotional environment.

Some patterns that were seen among patients of multiple sclerosis were: stressful or traumatic events between 6 months and 2 years before onset; a cumulative correlation between stress and relapse; histories of childhood trauma; physical and sexual abuse histories; being less in touch with their emotions; and social support mitigating the effect of life stresses.

Gabor says he is yet to find an exception to these general findings.

A recent study has shown that people with stress-related disorders have a significantly greater risk of autoimmune disease. The same has been found in experiments with mice.

Goal:

The fifth chapter of *The Myth of Normal* teaches us about autoimmune conditions. We get to know of real life cases that suffered from these conditions, the trauma that they faced growing up, and their path to recovery. We also learn about how grief and vexation can cause multiple sclerosis. The authors discuss the reason for the rise in autoimmune diseases.

Lesson:

Activity 1:
Reflect on self-compassion. We learn about how important it is to hold compassion for the self, especially if we are experiencing disease or stress.
Answer this question: How do you think your attitude and life might change if you responded to yourself in the same way you typically respond to someone you love when he or she is suffering?

Checklist:

Key learnings from this chapter are:
- [ ] Autoimmunity is the immune system's assault on the body it is supposed to defend.
- [ ] Autoimmune conditions are characterized by inflammation of the afflicted organs, tissues, and body parts.
- [ ] They are considered to be "idiopathic" in nature, which

means of unknown origin.
- Since the cause of autoimmune diseases has not been identified yet, it has not been possible for medicine to cure or reverse them.
- The first mystery around them is around why they are becoming more frequent. The second is their highly skewed gender distribution against women.
- The term "neurogenic inflammation" refers to stress-induced inflammation that gets triggered by discharges of the nervous system.
- Research has shown that early adversity can lead to inflammation in adult life.

Action Plan:

- Reflect on the idea of disease. Consider the possibility – what if disease is not a fixed entity but something dynamic, a process that expresses real life in concrete situations?

Are you enjoying the book so far?

If so, please help me reach more readers by taking 30 seconds to write just a few words on Amazon

Or, you can choose to leave one later...

Chapter 6: It Ain't a Thing: Disease as a Process

In the sixth chapter of *The Myth of Normal* by Gabor Maté and Daniel Maté, we get to know the abuse undergone by a woman from early childhood and her battle with uterine cancer. Gabor says that toxic self-blame is one of the torments experienced by the traumatized child.

The language we use to express our defiance against disease is like it's a battle to be won. These metaphors reflect our anger and despair. However, rather than being a battle, it is more of a push-pull phenomenon of finding balance and harmony.

Another view of disease that needs to be looked at from a different perspective is when we refer to it as something we got – "I have cancer." We separate ourselves and make ourselves distinct and independent from the disease. It becomes external, something with its own identity and nature that encroaches upon our lives.

We need to deal with illness like it is a process that cannot be separated from our personal histories and the context and culture in which we live. When we refuse to look at illness as something concrete and develop the willingness to look both within and without, we can start to exercise agency. We can shift from being victims to becoming active participants.

Our relationship with ourselves and our emotional dynamics are the most powerful determinants of our future. The more optimistic we are about recovery, the longer we survive. Gabor says there are no clear dividing lines between illness and health. No one suddenly falls sick.

While stress does not "cause" cancer, it keeps the immune system from successfully confronting the body's own internal threat to well-being.

Steve Cole, a leading British cancer physician, says that to get a disease, a whole series of things had to have gone wrong. Some of these could be genes, pathogen exposure, and just hard lives. When people feel threatened or insecure over an extended period of time, their bodies turn on inflammatory genes.

Goal:

The sixth chapter of *The Myth of Normal* talks about how disease is not a thing but a process. It is beyond the war metaphor – something to be battled against. We learn about the process of disease and how our relationship with ourselves is the most powerful determinant of our future.

Lesson:

Activity 1:
Think about your relationship with disease. Is it possible to look at illness as an imbalance in the entire organism, not just as a manifestation of molecules, cells, or organs invaded by pathology?

Activity 2:
Is it possible to apply the findings of Western research and medical science in a systems framework? When you look at a disease, can you map out all the connections and conditions that you think could have contributed to illness and health?

Checklist:

Key learnings from this chapter are:
- [ ] Toxic self-blame is one of the torments experienced by the traumatized child.
- [ ] Rather than being a battle, illness is more a push-pull phenomenon of finding balance and harmony.
- [ ] We need to deal with illness like it is a process that cannot be separated from our personal histories and the context and culture in which we live.
- [ ] When we refuse to look at illness as something concrete and

develop the willingness to look both within and without, we can start to exercise agency.

☐ Gabor says there are no clear dividing lines between illness and health. No one suddenly falls sick.

☐ When people feel threatened or insecure over an extended period of time, their bodies turn on inflammatory genes.

Action Plan:

☐ We learn about the possible implications of suppressing our emotions. Are there any emotions you are uncomfortable feeling? Do certain emotions evade you? Spend some time writing about the emotions that you experience most often, the ones that you feel are 'wrong' and should not be experienced, and the ones that you feel the least.

Chapter 7: A Traumatic Tension: Attachment vs. Authenticity

In the seventh chapter of *The Myth of Normal* by Gabor Maté and Daniel Maté, we are introduced to Anita Moorjani's story of being a people pleaser. She attributes developing cancer to chronic stress induced by the compulsive suppression of her own needs.

Gabor talks about how it is important to strike a balance between not blaming oneself for illness and asserting that features of one's personality contribute to the onset of illness. One needs to look at the bigger picture so there can be prevention and healing and ultimately, self-acceptance and self-forgiveness.

The belief that certain personality traits can pose risks for illness goes a long way. A tendency to be easily angered shows a link to heart disease. In Chinese medicine, the liver is associated with the emotions of anger, bitterness, and resentment. The type "C" personality has been associated with malignancy – being cooperative and appeasing, unassertive, patient, unexpressive of negative emotions, and compliant. Everything that describes 'pleasers'.

Gabor says that repression disarms one's ability to protect oneself from stress. It implies going through life being stressed while not knowing that you are stressed. As a result, one cannot do much to protect oneself from the long-term consequences of stress on the body and mind.

Psychologists have studied the physiological effects of suppression – consciously inhibiting one's emotional expressive behavior when emotionally aroused. The suppression group in the study, when shown films that would normally elicit disgust, showed heightened activation of their fight or flight nervous system, a stress response.

When a person deliberately chooses to not express how she is feeling and does it habitually or under compulsion, its effect is likely to be toxic.

We develop these habits of personality as coping patterns. The problem is that traits such as putting others first, not expressing our anger, overdrive, and a rigid identification with social role, duty, and responsibility are regarded as admirable strengths in our culture. They are confused for compassion, honor, diligence, temperance, conscience, and so forth. However, the latter qualities do not ask of us to suppress, overstep, or ignore who we are and what we need.

Psychologist Lydia Temoshok has pointed out that Type C is not a personality but a behavior pattern can that be changed. We are not born with those traits and hence can unlearn them.

Gabor talks about how there is a clash between two of our essential needs: attachment and authenticity. Attachment is our need for physical and emotional closeness. As infants, our need for attachment is mandatory. Even as adults, for many of us, our attachment circuits can override those of rationality, decision-making, and conscious will. The coping styles we develop to maintain our earliest attachment relationships form the template for how we approach all our significant relationships.

Authenticity is the quality of being true to oneself and then shaping one's life from a deep knowledge of that self. It is also rooted in survival instincts because it is knowing our gut feelings when they arise and then honoring them.

Children might feel while growing up that certain parts of them are accepted while others are not. This creates a split in the child's sense of self. A child inevitably picks the need for attachment over the need for authenticity because it needs to be cared for. This is not a conscious choice.

Our biggest need is that of survival. Survival as a child depends on the maintenance of attachment, whatever it may take, even authenticity. The outcome is predictable.

We might not have chosen authenticity as children. However, with awareness and self-compassion, we can move towards greater authenticity.

Goal:

The seventh chapter of *The Myth of Normal* talks about how compulsive suppression of one's own emotions and needs is the root of illness. We learn about attachment, authenticity, and the conflict between the two. There is also a discussion on the importance of striking a balance between not blaming oneself for illness and asserting that features of one's personality contribute to the onset of illness.

Lesson:

Activity 1:
In this chapter, we learn about the conflict between attachment and authenticity. Take some time to think about this and then write down your answer:
In what areas of your life do you think your need for attachment feels like it is threatened by your authenticity?

Checklist:

Key learnings from this chapter are:
- [ ] The type "C" personality has been associated with malignancy – being cooperative and appeasing, unassertive, patient, inexpressive of negative emotions, and compliant.
- [ ] Repression disarms one's ability to protect oneself from stress.
- [ ] When a person deliberately chooses to not express how she is feeling and does it habitually or under compulsion, its effect is likely to be toxic.

- The problem is that traits such as putting others first, not expressing our anger, overdrive, and a rigid identification with social role, duty, and responsibility are regarded as admirable strengths in our culture.
- There is a clash between two of our essential needs: attachment and authenticity.
- The coping styles we develop to maintain our earliest attachment relationships form the template for how we approach all our significant relationships.
- A child inevitably picks the need for attachment over the need for authenticity because it needs to be cared for.
- With awareness and self-compassion, we can move towards greater authenticity.

Action Plan:

☐ Write down 10 ways in which you can start being more authentic:

1.

2.

3.

4.

5.

6.

7.

8.

9.

10.

Chapter 8: Who Are We Really? Human Nature, Human Needs

The eighth chapter of *The Myth of Normal* by Gabor Maté and Daniel Maté begins with the question – what is our nature? Gabor says that he believes this question is central, with far-ranging implications.

The health of any life form is closely related to its essential needs being met or not met. We can only be who we are when we know what we need to be who we are. The identity that we give to ourselves determines how we set up our lives.

We often dismiss our manipulative, self-serving behavior by saying "it's human nature". Our culture is accustomed to seeing people as inherently aggressive, acquisitive, and individualistic. The qualities of kindness, charity, and community are seen as exceptions to a rule.

However, this is not true for every culture. There are cultures in which self-interest is looked upon with disdain. It is considered a loss of humanity.

Gabor says a fixed view of human nature is unhelpful and misleading. We can be anything: noble and narcissistic, brilliant and stupid, and generous and genocidal. Our nature is a range of possible outcomes. Different conditions bring out different versions of us. If we don't remain nimble to this understanding, we can make the mistake of believing that we are a particular kind of person and prevent ourselves from considering other possibilities.

How our nature develops depends on how our basic needs are met and how our potentials are treated. While this holds true throughout our lifespans, it is critical during the process of development. The conditions under which our development takes place determine whether our needs are met and our potentials are manifested.

The environment must satisfy our needs for us to flourish. We need to get over the myth that we are programmed to behave in certain ways. We are adaptable and have the capacity for intervention. However, we do not thrive in all kinds of environments, whether physical, emotional, or social.

One of our inherent needs is that of reciprocity. It is our neural expectancy. Gabor says that his working assumption is that caring, relative harmony, and equilibrium is our baseline nature. We thrive when these are present; we suffer when they are not.

A capitalist system is designed to make a competitive, individualized system as the normal. If normal is natural, it is the norm. And if it is the norm, it will endure. It undermines connectedness to others and normalizes selfishness.

Goal:

The eighth chapter of *The Myth of Normal* by Gabor Maté and Daniel Maté explores an existential question – what is our nature? Gabor says that he believes this question is central, with far-ranging implications. He says his working assumption is that caring, relative harmony, and equilibrium is our baseline nature. We thrive when these are present; we suffer when they are not.

Lesson:

Activity 1:
We are warned against adopting a fixed view of our natures. Instead, we are advised to ask: what circumstances evoke which sort of outcomes?
To better understand this, write one example for each of the instances when you have shown the following characteristics:
- Nobility:

- Narcissism:

- Generosity

- Selfishness

- Brilliance

- Stupidity

Checklist:

Key learnings from this chapter are:
- [ ] The health of any life form is closely related to its essential needs being met or not met.
- [ ] The identity that we give to ourselves determines how we set up our lives.
- [ ] Our culture is accustomed to seeing people as inherently aggressive, acquisitive, and individualistic. The qualities of kindness, charity, and community are seen as exceptions to a rule.
- [ ] A fixed view of human nature is unhelpful and misleading.
- [ ] Our nature is a range of possible outcomes. Different conditions bring out different versions of us.
- [ ] How our nature develops depends on how our basic needs are met and how our potentials are treated.
- [ ] The environment must satisfy our needs for us to flourish.
- [ ] One of our inherent needs is that of reciprocity. It is our neural expectancy.
- [ ] A capitalist system is designed to make a competitive, individualized system as the normal. It undermines connectedness to others and normalizes selfishness.

Action Plan:

☐ Think about a behavior you would like to change. Now answer the following questions:

1. Why do you want to make that change?

2. What would you be giving up if you stopped that behavior?

3. What is one step you can take to change that behavior?

Chapter 9: A Sturdy or Fragile Foundation: Children's Irreducible Needs

The ninth chapter of *The Myth of Normal* by Gabor Maté and Daniel Maté talks about how children's developmental needs are of urgent practical importance. Its individual and collective stakes are high.

Neuroscientist Antonio Damasio says that the homeostatic and emotional function of the brain develops months ahead of the thinking part of the brain. Because a child feels much before he thinks, it determines a lot about what kind of things he thinks when thinking becomes possible. Also, research has shown that early experience molds behavior, emotional patterns, unconscious beliefs, learning styles, relational dynamics, self-regulation, and the ability to handle stress.

Gabor says that early development sets the ground for all the learning, behavior, and health that come later. The analogy that Gabor uses is that if emotion is the ground of cognition and relationships are the tectonic plates that shape that ground. Emotion is the mind's primary architect.

Therefore, children's sense of security, trust in the world, interconnectedness, and connection to their authentic emotions depends on the emotional stability and availability of their parents.

The goal of parenting can be said to bring that child to his or her full potential as a human being. That goal is missed because of the failure to understand the needs of the developing child.

What children need first and foremost is the comfort that they can exist in our presence exactly the way they are. Parents need to communicate in every way to the child that the child is loved, welcomed, and wanted for precisely what he or she is. The child does not need to be or do something different to win that love. It does not depend on the child's behavior or personality. It is simply there.

What should one do when children behave in a way that is dangerous or unacceptable? Stopping that behavior needs to come from an unconditionally loving place. Children need the trust that nothing they might do is a threat to the relationship, even if it brings about momentary anger.

The one word that describes what children need is security. It comes from warm and attuned interactions with caregivers. Our optimal development requires that our social and emotional needs are met. In the absence of secure attachment, the emotions of Panic / Grief get activated.

The four irreducible or non-negotiable needs for human maturation are:

1. The attachment relationship: a child's deep sense of contact and connection with its caregivers

2. A sense of attachment security that allows the child to feel that it does not have to "win" love and allows the child to be who he is and as he is

3. Permission to feel one's emotions, especially anger, sadness, pain, and grief; the safety to be vulnerable

4. The experience of free play in order to mature

Goal:
The ninth chapter of *The Myth of Normal* talks about how children's developmental needs are of urgent practical importance. We learn about how early development of a child's brain happens, the importance of emotion over thought, and the goal of parenting and why it fails. The chapter ends with the four irreducible or non-negotiable needs for maturation.

Lesson:
Activity 1: In this chapter, we learn about childhood development. Think about your childhood experiences and write down 3 events that could have impacted your emotional development. 1. 2. 3.

Checklist:
Key learnings from this chapter are: ☐ Neuroscientist Antonio Damasio says that the homeostatic and emotional function of the brain develops months ahead of the thinking part of the brain. ☐ Because a child feels much before he thinks, it determines a lot about what kind of things he thinks when thinking becomes possible. ☐ Research has shown that early experience molds behavior, emotional patterns, unconscious beliefs, learning styles,

relational dynamics, self-regulation, and the ability to handle stress.
- ☐ Emotion is the mind's primary architect.
- ☐ Children's sense of security, trust in the world, interconnectedness, and connection to their authentic emotions depends on the emotional stability and availability of their parents.
- ☐ Parents need to communicate in every way to the child that the child is loved, welcomed, and wanted for precisely what he or she is.
- ☐ Children need the trust that nothing they might do is a threat to the relationship, even if it brings about momentary anger.
- ☐ Our optimal development requires that our social and emotional needs are met.
- ☐ In the absence of secure attachment, the emotions of Panic / Grief get activated.

Action Plan:

- ☐ Reflect on the four irreducible or non-negotiable needs for human maturation. If there is a child in your environment, assess if these needs are being met.

Chapter 10: Trouble at the Threshold: Before We Come into the World

The tenth chapter of *The Myth of Normal* by Gabor Maté and Daniel Maté begins with Gabor talking about how, before we become creators, we are creations. The world fashions us before we can take part in the construction of our universe. It does this through the bodies, minds, and circumstances of our parents.

Gabor says that we might not be able to recall our intrauterine experiences but they live on as emotional and neurological memory that gets embedded in our cells and nervous system. Psychiatrist Thomas Verny has called this "bodywide memory".

Science is increasingly recognizing the importance of women's physical environment, health, and emotional balance during pregnancy for the optimal development of the infant. With the increase in the number of children and young people experiencing depression, anxiety, and other mental health challenges, it is critical that we look to the environment.

The emotional, economic, personal, professional, and social stress that pregnant women are under is a very early factor in the development of the infant. The infant receives all of the anxieties, happiness, and difficulties of the parents.

Women need to be asked different questions during their prenatal checkups – about their mental and emotional states, and their stresses at home and / or work.

It has been reported that fetuses of mothers who are stressed or depressed respond differently from those of mothers who are emotionally healthy. These infants have a significantly higher risk of developing learning and behavioral problems and may be more prone to depression and anxiety as they age. Essential neurotransmitters like serotonin and dopamine are also affected.

It has also been seen that there are certain periods in development during which the fetus and later the infant is particularly vulnerable to the environment. Telomeres were seen to be shorter in twenty-five year old adults whose mothers faced major stress during pregnancy. High stress in mothers was also seen to impair the child's stress-response capabilities well into midlife. It was also seen to create intestinal problems and allergies in babies.

A survey has shown that paternal depression can elevate the risk of extreme prematurity and is also known to affect sperm quality.

Goal:

The tenth chapter of *The Myth of Normal* talks about how, before we become creators, we are creations. The world fashions us before we can take part in the construction of our universe. It does this through the bodies, minds, and circumstances of our parents.

Lesson:

Activity 1:
In this chapter, we learn about how important support is for our own emotional safety and balance. Write down 3 areas in which you could do with more support. See if you can express those needs to others.

1.

2.

3.

Checklist:

Key learnings from this chapter are:
- We might not be able to recall our intrauterine experiences but they live on as emotional and neurological memory that gets embedded in our cells and nervous system. Psychiatrist Thomas Verny has called this "bodywide memory".
- Science is increasingly recognizing the importance of women's physical environment, health, and emotional

balance during pregnancy for the optimal development of the infant.
- The emotional, economic, personal, professional, and social stress that pregnant women are under is a very early factor in the development of the infant.
- The infant receives all of the anxieties, happiness, and difficulties of the parents.
- It has been reported that fetuses of mothers who are stressed or depressed respond differently from those of mothers who are emotionally healthy.
- It has also been seen that there are certain periods in development during which the fetus and later the infant is particularly vulnerable to the environment.
- A survey has shown that paternal depression can elevate the risk of extreme prematurity and is also known to affect sperm quality.

Action Plan:

- If there is a pregnant woman in your environment, see if there are any ways in which you could provide support, whether physical, emotional, or social.

Chapter 11: What Choice Do I Have? Childbirth in a Medicalized Culture

The eleventh chapter of *The Myth of Normal* by Gabor Maté and Daniel Maté begins with Gabor sharing stories of how tribes and natives have used ancient and natural practices when it comes to childbirth. With the development of western medicine and procedures, these practices have either been lost or relegated to the background.

He says that present-day medical practice often contradicts the wisdom of Nature. Rather than dismissing age-old practices, we can learn from them and embrace both.

Women should not be passive recipients of medical care. It disrupts the physiological, hormonal, and psychological processes that ensure the necessary bonding of mother and baby.

Medical intervention should be employed when necessary to reduce risk, maximize health, and ensure survival. However, it has become the default approach. For example, about 10 to 15 percent of all deliveries need to be C-sections. Gabor says this number is 40 percent in his province of British Columbia.

Experts are now of the opinion that we need to rediscover midwifery. Medicine needs to be Nature's attendant, not its ruler. Research has also found that interventions in maternity care can disturb hormonal processes, reduce their benefits, and create new and different challenges.

Gabor says there are two reasons for women losing control over their bodies during childbirth: One is that there is systemic sexism against women. The second is the western medical view of distrusting natural processes and fear of what can or may go wrong.

We need a healthcare system that honors women's strengths and vulnerabilities because it gives them the best chance at a childbirth experience. The most positive are the ones in which women feel they understood all the decisions that were made and had a say in the decision-making.

Birth prepares the template for the mother and child relationship. This relationship is the locus of the child's early development. A 2019 World Health Organization report says that 42 percent of women experienced physical or verbal abuse or discrimination during childbirth in health centers.

Goal:

The eleventh chapter of *The Myth of Normal* begins with Gabor sharing stories of how tribes and natives have used ancient and natural practices when it comes to childbirth. With the development of western medicine and procedures, these practices have either been lost or relegated to the background. We learn about the importance of trusting nature in its processes and women with their bodies.

Lesson:

Activity 1:
Think about the ways in which you could respect and take care of your body a bit more:

1.

2.

3.

4.

5.

Checklist:

Key learnings from this chapter are:
- [ ] Present-day medical practice often contradicts the wisdom of Nature. Rather than dismissing age-old practices, we can learn from them and embrace both.
- [ ] Women should not be passive recipients of medical care. It disrupts the physiological, hormonal, and psychological

processes that ensure the necessary bonding of mother and baby.

☐ Medical intervention should be employed when necessary to reduce risk, maximize health, and ensure survival. However, it has become the default approach.

☐ Medicine needs to be Nature's attendant, not its ruler.

☐ Research has also found that interventions in maternity care can disturb hormonal processes, reduce their benefits, and create new and different challenges.

☐ We need a healthcare system that honors women's strengths and vulnerabilities because it gives them the best chance at a childbirth experience.

☐ Birth prepares the template for the mother and child relationship. This relationship is the locus of the child's early development.

Action Plan:

☐ Speak with someone who has given birth recently and try and understand the experience that they went through.

Chapter 12: Horticulture on the Moon: Parenting, Undermined

The twelfth chapter of *The Myth of Normal* by Gabor Maté and Daniel Maté talks about how we are flooded with parenting advice. There are innumerable books, blogs, and groups to help moms and dads with everything from conception through college drop-offs.

Good parenting can feel like a battle. We want to be the best parents and do the right things. We just don't know how.

As humans, we are naturally endowed with an innate drive and talent for child rearing. However, society's assumptions and prejudices alienate us from that natural knowledge.

The flaw as Gabor sees it is that parents have started taking their cues from a culture that is no longer in touch with both: the child's developmental needs and what parents require to be able to meet those needs.

Gabor shares some history of child rearing attitudes from the past. He talks about infanticide, terror, and abuse that were normalized in their day.

The 14th century was intent on breaking the independent spirit of the child and it was during this time that parenting manuals began to appear. The mid 19th century was about creating the socializing mode, the goal of which was to foster a socially functional personality, one that conformed to society's expectations. Most experts on parenting would have us ignore the child's developmental needs that come from our innate parenting instinct.

There is evidence to support the belief that when a baby is both and for months thereafter, a mother's need for contact is more than that of the infant. There are built-in physiological and emotional incentives for the caregivers or else parenthood would not have been possible. It has been seen that a baby's smile lights up the same reward areas in the mother's brain as junk foods or addictive drugs, releasing the same pleasure chemicals and giving the same high.

In 2018, the American Academy of Pediatrics issued a statement calling for an end to spanking and harsh verbal punishment for children and adolescents. They said that such treatment was responsible for increasing aggression in the long-term and undermining the development of self-control and responsibility. It could also cause harm to healthy brain development and lead to mental health problems.

The more stressed the parent, the more stressed the child. When parents are stressed, they are less patient, more punishing, and harsher with their children. Stress negatively affects their capacity to be calm, responsive, and attuned. It also shows up as distraction and emotional absence.

The more support parents receive, the more responsive they can be to their children.

Goal:

The twelfth chapter of *The Myth of Normal* talks about how we are flooded with parenting advice and yet parenting can feel like a battle. This is because we do not trust our natural drive and talent for child rearing. Society's assumptions and prejudices alienate us from that natural knowledge. Gabor also shares with us some child rearing practices from the past.

Lesson:

Activity 1:
This list is of 7 early childbearing practices. Compare these with the experiences of the average baby or toddler of our time:
1. Soothing perinatal experience
2. Prompt responsiveness to the needs of the infant and prevention of distress
3. Extensive touch and constant physical presence, including touch with movement
4. Frequent, infant-initiated breastfeeding for two to five years, with four as the average weaning age
5. A community of multiple, warm, responsive adult caregivers
6. A climate of positive social support
7. Creative free play in nature with multi-aged mates

Checklist:

Key learnings from this chapter are:
- [ ] Parents have started taking their cues from a culture that is no longer in touch with both: the child's developmental needs and what parents require to be able to meet those needs.
- [ ] The 14th century was intent on breaking the independent spirit of the child and it was during this time that parenting manuals began to appear.

- The mid 19th century was about creating the socializing mode, the goal of which was to foster a socially functional personality, one that conformed to society's expectations.
- There are built-in physiological and emotional incentives for the caregivers or else parenthood would not have been possible.
- When parents are stressed, they are less patient, more punishing, and harsher with their children.
- The more support parents receive, the more responsive they can be to their children.

Action Plan:

- We do not usually associate the word "dignity" when it comes to children. Even babies know when their physical and emotional integrity are being violated. Can you associate with this word and think of children with regard to their dignity?

Chapter 13: Forcing the Brain in the Wrong Direction: The Sabotage of Childhood

The thirteenth chapter of *The Myth of Normal* by Gabor Maté and Daniel Maté begins with a discussion on how parents are responsible for their children and yet they do not alone create the world in which they have to parent them.

The destabilization of parenting begins with stress being transmitted to the fetus itself. It then proceeds to the mechanization of birth and then the denial of the child's developmental needs. The economic and social pressure on parents and the erosion of community ties magnifies this. This ends with the exploitation of children and youth by the consumer market.

As parents, the ability to child rear is heavily influenced by the parents' own early experiences, unresolved traumas, social expectations, and stresses of life. Some of the things that make an environment socially hazardous for a child are violence, poverty, economic pressures, relationship disruptions, nastiness, despair, depression, paranoia, and alienation.

Children *need* to attach to someone in their lives. When they do not find a reliable figure, they experience fear and disorientation. Their learning, social interaction, and emotional regulation also do not develop appropriately.

When there is an attachment void, children find the next available person, which, in most cases, is their peer group. They start seeking acceptance from one another. Forming close relationships with peers is otherwise healthy and natural. However, when this happens because of replacement, it is disastrous. Once this happens, kids lose the safety of the primary connection with adults.

In the absence of spending time with caring adults, children are compelled to choose between two competing attachments, that of parental connection and their peer world. This is a sign of coping for children and cannot be looked upon as hopeful because the peer group cannot provide an abiding connection that children's development safety demands. At its best, a peer group can offer conditional acceptance, thus fostering insecurity, self-suppression, and conformity. At worst, it exposes children to rejection, ostracization, and bullying.

In an unsafe atmosphere of bullying, peer rejection, or mockery, a child shuts down her vulnerable emotions as a protective response. The running away from vulnerability inhibits maturation. There is a significant loss of feeling. This reinforces a sense of emptiness. It fosters boredom, impairs genuine intimacy, and drives a compulsion for overstimulation.

Our emotions have critical survival value. They are an indispensable part of who we are. We can be either in defensive mode or in growth mode. We cannot be in both at the same time.

The neurological effects of screen watching on children include language delay, poor sleep, impaired executive function and general cognition, and decreased parent-child engagement. Consumerism and screen culture is causing free play, one of the irreducible needs of childhood, to be sacrificed.

Goal:
The thirteenth chapter of *The Myth of Normal* talks about the culture that kids grow up in. It discusses a child's need for secure adult attachment and how, when that need is not met, children look towards their peer group for that support and approval. This can be detrimental to the development of the child. We also learn how consumerism and screen time negatively impact children.

Lesson:
Activity 1: We learn how clever marketing engages children in the most fundamental emotions: love (nurturing, affection, romance), fear (violence, terror, cruelty, war), and mastery (kids' aspiration to get independence from adults). Think about any recent advertisements that you have seen for kids and try and assess which of our emotions they engage.

Checklist:
Key learnings from this chapter are: ☐ The destabilization of parenting begins with stress being transmitted to the fetus itself. ☐ It then proceeds to the mechanization of birth and then the denial of the child's developmental needs. ☐ As parents, the ability to child rear is heavily influenced by the parents' own early experiences, unresolved traumas, social expectations, and stresses of life. ☐ Children *need* to attach to someone in their lives. When they do not find a reliable figure, they experience fear and disorientation. ☐ When there is an attachment void, children find the next available person, which, in most cases, is their peer group. They start seeking acceptance from one another. ☐ In the absence of spending time with caring adults, children

are compelled to choose between two competing attachments, that of parental connection and their peer world.

☐ This is a sign of coping for children and cannot be looked upon as hopeful because the peer group cannot provide an abiding connection that children's development safety demands.

☐ In an unsafe atmosphere of bullying, peer rejection, or mockery, a child shuts down her vulnerable emotions as a protective response.

☐ The neurological effects of screen watching on children include language delay, poor sleep, impaired executive function and general cognition, and decreased parent-child engagement.

Action Plan:

☐ We learn about the importance of praising a child's effort and not valuing only their achievement. Try and incorporate this in your interactions with children.

Chapter 14: A Template for Distress: How Culture Builds Our Character

The fourteenth chapter of *The Myth of Normal* by Gabor Maté and Daniel Maté begins with Gabor comparing humans, in their lack of an independently self-determined self, to ants.

Ants follow a caste system. While all are born with virtually the same set of genes, what they become depends entirely on the need of the clan. Much like ants, we have far less autonomy than we would like to believe. The character and personalities we develop reflect the needs of our social environment.

The nuclear family is held within a larger context such as community, neighborhood, city, economy, country, and so on. There is an authenticity/attachment conflict here too. We are groomed to fulfill our expected social roles and adopt the characteristics needed to do so, irrespective of the cost to our well-being.

Our identity crises are not consciously manufactured. They are the outcome of how we develop in all these different contexts, starting from the family and moving outward. The collective "we" is blind and dangerous. It normalizes injustices and calamities. It is as if we are hypnotized into compliance. The values of the system that we inhabit and its expectations get under our skin in a way that we start confusing them with ours.

Here are some of the features of the social character that we imbue in our culture:

1. Separation from Self: Some traits are acquired, for example, excessive identification with socially imposed duty at the expense of one's own needs. This is a result of a child's development needs being denied. They are made concrete through society's reinforcement and reward e.g. workaholism.

2. Consumption Hunger: We have been conditioned to believe that what we want is what we need. Our consumerist society takes desire for need. When we fail to achieve what we desire, we look at it as personal failure. Our conviction of insufficiency makes us addicts to consumption.

3. Hypnotic Passivity: We start regimenting children very early on. Society is designed to reduce, mollify, and limit the efforts of a child and control its destiny.

Goal:

The fourteenth chapter of *The Myth of Normal* discusses society and its role in shaping a child's character and controlling its destiny. We learn about the three features of the social character that we imbue in our culture: separation from self, consumption hunger, and hypnotic passivity.

Lesson:

Activity 1:
We learn about 'separation from self'. Think and write down ways in which societal expectations could have shaped your habits and behavior.

1.

2.

3.

Checklist:

Key learnings from this chapter are:
- [ ] Ants follow a caste system. While all are born with virtually the same set of genes, what they become depends entirely on the need of the clan. Much like ants, we have far less autonomy than we would like to believe.
- [ ] The character and personalities we develop reflect the needs of our social environment.
- [ ] We are groomed to fulfill our expected social roles and adopt the characteristics needed to do so, irrespective of the cost to our well-being.

- Our identity crises are not consciously manufactured.
- They are the outcome of how we develop in all these different contexts, starting from the family and moving outward.
- The collective "we" is blind and dangerous. It normalizes injustices and calamities.

Action Plan:

- Consumerism is founded on creating a feeling of insufficiency. Think about all the things that you feel you need but are actually just desires.
  1.
  2.
  3.
  4.
  5.

Chapter 15: Just Not to Be You: Debunking the Myths About Addiction

The fifteenth chapter of *The Myth of Normal* by Gabor Maté and Daniel Maté starts with a story about addiction.

There are two leading misconceptions about addiction: it is either the product of 'bad choices' or else a disease. Both fail to explain and cure this social plague.

Gabor says that he is yet to meet anyone who ever "chose" to become addicted. Recent studies have shown that repeated drug use causes long-lasting changes in the brain that inhibit voluntary control. There is loss of free will. He goes on to say that most addicted people had little choice even before they developed the habit. Their brains were already impaired by their life experiences.

The disease assumption misses the body mind connection. Personal and social life events shape the brain throughout the lifetime. Substances that create dependence change the brain over time so that essential functions like impulse regulation become significantly compromised. The same can happen with internet games and foods that trigger the brain's reward mechanism.

To understand addiction, we need to consider their experiences with the world. Addictions are rooted in coping mechanisms. They can take on some of the features of disease, such as a dysfunctional organ, tissue damage, physical symptoms, cycles of remission and relapse, and even death. They represent the defenses of a person against suffering he/she does not know how to endure. It is an attempt to soothe the injuries of childhood and stresses of adulthood.

Addictions, at least at their onset, provide for some essential human need. They also provide some form of social connection. Addiction's benefits can be summarized as an escape from the prison of the self. It helps one flee from the mundane, isolated, and uncomfortable sense of being with oneself. That discomfort comes from a feeling of being abnormal, unworthy, and deficient.

Addiction calls to us when our normal, day-to-day life seems like a suffering. Pain is the central theme. Addiction then is like anesthesia. It is a call for self-escape.

The question then to ask is not why the addiction but why the pain.

Goal:
The fifteenth chapter of *The Myth of Normal* introduces us to addiction. It debunks the two most common assumptions about addiction – that it is a result of bad choices and that it is a disease. Gabor helps us understand addiction better. He also guides us on what questions to ask about addiction.

Lesson:
Activity 1: If you are struggling with any kind of addiction, ask yourself the following questions: - What is "right" about the addiction? - What benefit are you deriving from it? - What does it do for you? - What are you getting that you otherwise cannot access?

Checklist:

Key learnings from this chapter are:
- [ ] Recent studies have shown that repeated drug use causes long-lasting changes in the brain that inhibit voluntary control.
- [ ] Most addicted people had little choice even before they developed the habit. Their brains were already impaired by their life experiences.
- [ ] Substances that create dependence change the brain over time so that essential functions like impulse regulation become significantly compromised.
- [ ] Addictions are rooted in coping mechanisms.
- [ ] It is an attempt to soothe the injuries of childhood and stresses of adulthood.
- [ ] Addictions, at least at their onset, provide for some essential human need. They also provide some form of social connection.
- [ ] Addiction calls to us when our normal, day-to-day life seems like a suffering. Pain is the central theme.

Action Plan:

- [ ] Has anyone around you struggled with addiction? If yes, you can use this chapter to build more empathy towards them by reflecting on how easy it can be to fall prey to something and how hard to come out of it.

Chapter 16: Show of Hands: A New View of Addiction

In the sixteenth chapter of *The Myth of Normal* by Gabor Maté and Daniel Maté, Gabor presents us with his definition of addiction:

"Addiction is a complex psychological, emotional, physiological, neurobiological, social, and spiritual process. It manifests through any behavior in which a person finds temporary relief or pleasure and therefore craves, but that in the long term causes them or others negative consequences, and yet the person refuses or is unable to give it up."

Addiction is not restricted to drugs. It covers compulsive sexual roving, pornography, internet, shopping, gaming, gambling, binge eating or drinking, purging, work, extreme sports, exercising, relationship-seeking, psychedelics, and meditation.

Not all addictions are created equal. Some people could have had diminished inner or outer resources available to them, faced socioeconomic and racial challenges, and undergone ostracization and punishment. These differences of degree matter and cannot be flattened or erased.

Gabor says addiction spares no one. Most of us who consider ourselves 'normal' bear enough resemblance to those we consider dependent. He reminds us of the small-t trauma and how trauma is about what happens inside us and not to us. Most of us will be able to locate ourselves somewhere on the trauma/psychological injury spectrum.

We tend to recall our happy memories and suppress awareness of emotional suffering.

All addictions, Gabor says, are a refugee story. It starts from intolerable feelings gone through during adversity, never processing them, and then moving into a state of temporary freedom even if it is unreal.

A study showed that the more adversity a child had been exposed to, the greater the risk of addictions, mental health issues, and other medical problems. Adversity has three subheadings: abuse (psychological, physical, sexual); neglect (physical, emotional); household dysfunction (loss of a parent, alcoholism or drug use in the home, depression or mental illness in the home, divorce, mother treated violently, imprisoned household member).

Any substance in itself is not addictive. What certain substances do is provide a desirable psychoactive relief.

Experiences of stress while in the womb can predispose one to addiction. They can impact the incentive-motivation system of the brain, which is impaired in all addictions.

All addictions involve dopamine – the brain's essential neurotransmitter in the motivation system. Addiction, at least in the beginning, is an attempt to induce feelings that should have generated in us naturally had we developed healthily.

Goal:

The sixteenth chapter of *The Myth of Normal* takes us further into understanding addiction. Gabor defines addiction for us and convinces us how we are all victims. We learn about how addictions develop, how they help us cope, and how we can be unequipped to help ourselves and stop.

Lesson:

Activity 1:
Are you craving or participating in something that provides you temporary relief or pleasure, inviting or incurring negative consequences? But you are not able to give it up.

Checklist:

Key learnings from this chapter are:
- ☐ Addiction is not restricted to drugs. It can cover other substances and behaviors.
- ☐ Most of us who consider ourselves 'normal' bear enough resemblance to those we consider dependent.
- ☐ We tend to recall our happy memories and suppress awareness of emotional suffering.
- ☐ All addictions are a refugee story. It starts from intolerable feelings gone through during adversity, never processing them, and then moving into a state of temporary freedom even if it is unreal.
- ☐ A study showed that the more adversity a child had been exposed to, the greater the risk of addictions, mental health issues, and other medical problems.
- ☐ Any substance in itself is not addictive. What certain substances do is provide a desirable psychoactive relief.
- ☐ All addictions involve dopamine – the brain's essential neurotransmitter in the motivation system.

Action Plan:

- ☐ This chapter shares poignant real life stories that show us how easy it is for anyone to get addicted to something. Take some time and reflect if there are any habits or things that you compulsively engage in or over-consume. If any come up, write them down.

Chapter 17: An Inaccurate Map of Our Pain: What We Get Wrong About Mental Illness

The seventeenth chapter of *The Myth of Normal* by Gabor Maté and Daniel Maté talks about how mainstream psychiatry reduces mental illness mostly to an imbalance in the DNA-dictated brain chemicals.

Gabor says that in his entire experience of dealing with mental illness, including his own, he has always found enough in people's personal histories to account for their mental and emotional suffering.

The term "mental illness" emphasizes brain physiology and implies that the problem falls within the domain of medicine. These assumptions limit our understanding. They are also harmful in the sense that they leave people subject to incomplete and inappropriate treatments and they come in the way of more humane, complete, and helpful treatments. It also takes away agency and power from the one who is suffering and now has to passively receive treatment, sometimes for a lifetime.

There are no ways to measure mental illness. In the absence of any measurable markers, the only data available is a subjective assessment of a person's own mood and their behaviors in terms of say sleep patterns, appetite, etc.

The concept of mental illness is a construct. It is a frame we have developed to understand a phenomenon and our understanding of it. It is definitely not objective.

Gabor believes that a diagnosis like depression or bipolar disorder does not explain anything. Diagnoses are summaries that are sometimes helpful but always incomplete. A diagnosis can help a person suffering in the way that it helps them account for and validate what they have been experiencing.

That said, the problem with diagnosis is that it can be believed to be an explanation. It's a circular argument. Why does someone have mood swings? It is because they have bipolar disorder. How does one know they have bipolar disorder? It is because they have mood swings.

The diagnostic system keeps our focus on the effects and not on the many causes. In his work, Gabor says that his focus is on the specific challenges that the person is facing in their lives and the trauma that is coming to life because of those challenges.

Medication does help. It can be life enhancing and even life saving. However, one has to be careful not to attribute the origin of mental illness to the biochemistry of the brain. Because the brain stores our personal narrative, difficult experiences can disturb its neurobiology.

It has been established that the greater the degree of childhood diversity, the higher the risk of mental disturbances, including psychosis. What can most powerfully predict a person's present functioning is their current relational connectedness and the second most powerful predictor is their history of connectedness.

Our genes may make some of us more vulnerable and sensitive to life's changes. Those of us who are sensitive feel more, feel more deeply, and are more easily overwhelmed by stress both subjectively and physiologically.

Those of us who feel more pain will have a greater need to escape through mental illness or addiction. They are more likely to zone out, dissociate, or develop fantasies. These same people are also unusually vital, creative, and successful when their environment is supportive and nurturing. They thrive under positive circumstances, with mental resilience and happiness. They are potentially more aware, insightful, inventive, artistic, and empathetic. It is both a gift and a curse.

No gene has ever been identified that causes mental illness. Professor Jehannine Austin, an academic and researcher who runs a genetic counseling clinic, says that what separates those who suffer from those who don't is what happens to them during their lives.

If we cling to the gene theory in order to avoid personal responsibility, we disempower ourselves from dealing with our suffering. We can take responsibility without feeling guilt or shame. It will help us stop feeling like victims.

Goal:

The seventeenth chapter of *The Myth of Normal* talks to us about the problems associated with the term mental illness and its diagnosis. We learn that there is no gene that causes mental illness. It all comes down to what we experience during our lives. Gabor talks about the need to take personal responsibility so we can feel empowered to help ourselves and not feel like victims of something that is outside of our control.

Lesson:

Activity 1:
We learn about how our culture disrupts healthy adult-child relationships. This is an exercise in self-reflection. Think about the ways in which instead of diagnosing a child, you can "diagnose" and treat a child's environment, under the following heads:
Family:

Community:

School:

Society:

Checklist:

Key learnings from this chapter are:
- [ ] The term "mental illness" emphasizes brain physiology and implies that the problem falls within the domain of medicine.
- [ ] There are no ways to measure mental illness. In the absence of any measurable markers, the only data available is a subjective assessment of a person's own mood and their behaviors in terms of say sleep patterns, appetite, etc.
- [ ] The concept of mental illness is a construct. It is a frame we have developed to understand a phenomenon and our understanding of it.
- [ ] A diagnosis can help a person suffering in the way that it helps them account for and validate what they have been experiencing.
- [ ] The diagnostic system keeps our focus on the effects and not on the many causes.
- [ ] Medication does help. It can be life enhancing and even life saving. However, one has to be careful not to attribute the origin of mental illness to the biochemistry of the brain.
- [ ] What can most powerfully predict a person's present functioning is their current relational connectedness and the second most powerful predictor is their history of connectedness.
- [ ] Those of us who are sensitive feel more, feel more deeply, and are more easily overwhelmed by stress both subjectively and physiologically.
- [ ] No gene has ever been identified that causes mental illness.

Action Plan:

- [ ] Have you ever said or thought about someone, "Don't be so sensitive." After reading this chapter, is it possible to have a fresh perspective on how some people can feel more sensitive to their environment and to change?

Chapter 18: The Mind Can Do Some Amazing Things: From Madness to Meaning

The eighteenth chapter of *The Myth of Normal* by Gabor Maté and Daniel Maté begins with Gabor's perspective on what mental illness is. He says it should be considered from the perspective of what it might be expressing about the life in which it arises.

There are stories that the authors share of people who were diagnosed with different kinds of mental illnesses. Sometimes multiple. All of them, without exception, had a troubled childhood. Their healing journeys were centered on finding meaning in their suffering. Many of those people could get off medication and lead healthy lives.

Something else that is nearly universal in people with mental health diagnoses and addictions is a belief in one's unworthiness. This begins as a coping mechanism to process life experiences.

A child who experiences early hurt adapts to be in a state of hyperalert fear, even when there is no immediate danger. The brain cannot discern between major and minor threats, or even no threat. The brain's capacity to recognize safety or threat evolves in a healthy way when there is a feeling of safety but gets disrupted when there is prolonged early insecurity. This disruption can result in feeling threatened when there is no threat or remaining oblivious even when there is danger.

Behaviors like self-harming play the role of self-soothing. They provide short-term relief and originate as an attempt to regulate our nervous system.

Gabor then talks about schizophrenia – widely believed to be a brain disease rooted in genetics, marked by psychoses, delusions, and hallucinations. He says no 'schizophrenia gene' has ever been found. He says what is being transmitted is the sensitivity and not the disease.

We use self-fragmentation as a defense when we feel that we cannot endure the experience. A way to escape that agony is to disconnect whenever the distressing emotions are triggered. Splitting from the present is an instantaneous self-defense in the midst of trauma.

An extreme form of flight from reality is disintegration that happens in psychosis. There is complete detachment from the here and now. A milder form of this is dissociation. In ADHD (attention deficit hyperactivity disorder) there is a chronic, reflexive tuning out. There is disconnection from the self, from one's activities, and from other people in disruptive ways.

In eating disorders, there is a desperate drive to get control at least over one's own body amid turmoil. There is a lack of control, identity, and self-worth, and a need to numb the pain. This takes the shape of seeking perfection via the body and self.

Goal:

The eighteenth chapter of *The Myth of Normal* offers us perspective on mental illness. The authors talk about how a mental illness should be seen from the view of what it might be expressing about the life in which it arises. A few cases are shared and we see how all of them have something to do with childhood adversities. There is also a discussion on mental health challenges like schizophrenia, ADHD, and eating disorders.

Lesson:

Activity 1:
This chapter urges us to visit our past. Take out some quiet time and think about what seemed difficult or challenging while growing up. Whether it was a situation or a more deep-seated fear, make a list of everything that comes up.

Activity 2:
After finishing the first activity, now think about the coping mechanisms that you used to avoid the discomfort when feeling that fear. What are the distractions that you employed so you can avoid that moment? Write all of them down.

Checklist:

Key learnings from this chapter are:
- Something else that is nearly universal in people with mental health diagnoses and addictions is a belief in one's unworthiness. This begins as a coping mechanism to process life experiences.
- A child who experiences early hurt adapts to be in a state of hyperalert fear, even when there is no immediate danger.
- The brain's capacity to recognize safety or threat gets disrupted when there is prolonged early insecurity and can result in feeling threatened when there is no threat or remaining oblivious even when there is danger.
- Behaviors like self-harming play the role of self-soothing. They provide short-term relief and originate as an attempt to regulate our nervous system.
- We use self-fragmentation as a defense when we feel that we cannot endure the experience.

Action Plan:

- Create pockets in the day where you can be without any distractions. Take this time to be with yourself with your phone and other disturbances away. Practice some deep breathing and if anything comes up for you that feels difficult, gently acknowledge it. Try to go within to find out what is causing this strong emotion. Over time, you will feel more comfortable with the discomfort.

Chapter 19: From Society to Cell: Uncertainty, Conflict, and Loss of Control

The nineteenth chapter of *The Myth of Normal* by Gabor Maté and Daniel Maté begins with a discussion on chronic stress and how it puts the nervous system on edge, distorts the hormonal system, reduces immunity, promotes inflammation, and negatively impacts physical and mental well-being.

Our most important stressors are emotional. The main determinants range from the personal to the cultural.

Stress creates an "allostatic load", the wear and tear of the body because of having to maintain internal equilibrium while undergoing changing and challenging circumstances. Our society leaves some people far more burdened than others, with the politically disempowered and economically disenfranchised having to bear much more allostatic stress.

Gabor says the most widespread emotional triggers for stress are uncertainty, conflict, lack of control, and lack of information. Capitalism breeds these conditions.

Capitalism provides us an ethic for us how we should behave, educate our children, and think. It is based on the tenet that economic growth is the supreme good. The western health system is also a reflection of that, where we look at life and health in purely individualistic terms.

We have to look at broad economic and political conditions to get perspective on individual health and happiness. Ignoring that is a core feature of materialism.

Culture affects all our biopsychosocial pathways, including epigenetic causes, stress-induced inflammation, premature aging, how and what we eat, and the toxins we ingest or inhale. It affects us through our parents, from one person to another, and from social, economic, and political conditions to individual bodies. It also powerfully influences and constrains all our individual decision with regard to our well-being.

Any stressor is a representation of the absence or threatened loss of something we perceive necessary for our survival, for example, love, work, dignity, self-esteem, or meaning.

Lower cortisol levels can be a marker of long-term stress. It is a sign that one's stress response mechanism is burning out. It often bodes future disease. Insecurity about work can instigate disease. It raises the risk of heart attacks, cigarettes, alcohol, and hypertension.

The more stress, threat, or uncertainty one experiences, the more the body turns on the defense mechanism of inflammation.

Accomplished economists, businessmen, and thought leaders have talked about how the political and economic system is failing our society and creating inequality.

Goal:

The nineteenth chapter of *The Myth of Normal* discusses how society and culture create biopsychosocial stress. Chronic stress puts the nervous system on edge, distorts the hormonal system, reduces immunity, promotes inflammation, and negatively impacts physical and mental well-being.

Lesson:

Activity 1:
In contrast to the short-lived rewards that are generated by food, alcohol, or self-destructive patterns of behavior, there are some activities we may undertake which have longer-term feelings of contentment. Which areas of your life can make you feel more content and in a better place to nurture a better worldview?

Checklist:

Key learnings from this chapter are:
- Our most important stressors are emotional. The main determinants range from the personal to the cultural.
- Stress creates an "allostatic load", the wear and tear of the body because of having to maintain internal equilibrium while undergoing changing and challenging circumstances.
- The most widespread emotional triggers for stress are uncertainty, conflict, lack of control, and lack of information. Capitalism breeds these conditions.
- Capitalism provides us an ethic for us how we should behave,

educate our children, and think. It is based on the tenet that economic growth is the supreme good.

- Culture affects all our biopsychosocial pathways, including epigenetic causes, stress-induced inflammation, premature aging, how and what we eat, and the toxins we ingest or inhale.
- Any stressor is a representation of the absence or threatened loss of something we perceive necessary for our survival, for example, love, work, dignity, self-esteem, or meaning.
- Lower cortisol levels can be a marker of long-term stress. It is a sign that one's stress response mechanism is burning out.

Action Plan:

- If you feel you have built a negative or stressful worldview, think back to your childhood and reflect on how your needs were met by your parents.

Chapter 20: Robbing the Human Spirit: Disconnection and Its Discontents

The twentieth chapter of *The Myth of Normal* by Gabor Maté and Daniel Maté begins with Gabor talking about the indispensability of connection. The negative health impacts of the absence of connection are immeasurable.

In a capitalist culture, acquisition takes precedence over qualities like love, trust, caring, social conscience, and engagement. Disease comes from people starting to lose a sense of meaning and experience disconnection.

Psychologists have listed our core needs as:

- Belonging, relatedness, connectedness
- Autonomy: a sense of control in one's life
- Mastery or competence
- Genuine and unconditional self-esteem
- Trust: a sense of having the personal and social resources that we need to sustain through life
- Purpose, meaning, transcendence

Bruce Alexander, author and professor of psychology talks about psychosocial integration. He says it is the marriage of our two basic needs – the need for social belonging and the need for individual autonomy and achievement.

Dislocation is a loss of connection to oneself, to others, and to a sense of meaning and purpose. The experience can be extremely painful. The same is true for social dislocation where large groups of people find themselves disconnected from autonomy, relatedness, trust, and meaning. This can be a source of mental dysfunction, despair, addictions, and physical illness.

Work brings together several of our core needs, including competence, mastery, and a sense of purpose. However, for most of us, work is a depleting and dispiriting experience. We are bound to experience alienation when our inner sense of value becomes status-driven and we rely on acceptance from others.

Meaning is a core need and an inherent expectation. Its absence and denial have severe consequences. Our hormones and nervous system also respond to its presence and absence. The more meaningful one perceives their life, the better one's measures of physical and mental health.

Rising loneliness is a public health crisis. It makes a person irritable, depressed, and self-centered. Chronic loneliness is associated with a risk of illness and early death.

The more insecure people feel, the more they focus on the material. While materialism promises satisfaction, it delivers hollow dissatisfaction. With increase in materialistic concerns, pro-social values like empathy, generosity, and cooperation take a backseat. It also leads to lower inter-personal relationships.

Goal:
The twentieth chapter of *The Myth of Normal* talks to us about disconnection – alienation, loneliness, loss of meaning, and dislocation. The authors tell us how disconnection promotes and is responsible for us becoming more addicted, chronically ill, and mentally disordered than ever before.

Lesson:
Activity 1: We learn about our core needs. Check your own experience and answer the following questions: What is it like when each of your core needs is met?   What happens in your mind and body when a core need is lacking, denied, or withdrawn?

Checklist:

Key learnings from this chapter are:
- [ ] The health impacts of the absence of connection are immeasurable.
- [ ] In a capitalist culture, acquisition takes precedence over qualities like love, trust, caring, social conscience, and engagement.
- [ ] Disease comes from people starting to lose a sense of meaning and experience disconnection.
- [ ] Psychosocial integration is the marriage of our two basic needs – the need for social belonging and the need for individual autonomy and achievement.
- [ ] Dislocation is a loss of connection to oneself, to others, and to a sense of meaning and purpose.
- [ ] Work brings together several of our core needs, including competence, mastery, and a sense of purpose. However, for most of us, work is a depleting and dispiriting experience.
- [ ] The more insecure people feel, the more they focus on the material.
- [ ] With increase in materialistic concerns, pro-social values like empathy, generosity, and cooperation take a backseat.

Action Plan:

- [ ] A question for self-reflection: When do you feel happier and more fulfilled and more at ease? When you extend yourself to help and connect with others or when you are focusing on catering to your little egoic self?

Chapter 21: They Just Don't Care If It Kills You: Sociopathy as Strategy

The twenty-first chapter of *The Myth of Normal* by Gabor Maté and Daniel Maté discusses how major corporations target the brain circuits of pleasure and reward to foster addictive compulsions.

The field called neuromarketing aims to market happiness but what it is actually selling is pleasure. Pleasure and happiness employ different neurochemicals: pleasure works with dopamine and opiates, both of which are short-term; contentment works on serotonin, which is more of a steady and slow release.

It is very hard to get addicted to anything serotonin – both substances and behaviors. Addictions control the dopamine (incentive/motivation) and opiate (pleasure/reward) systems of the brain. Pleasure without contentment and in the form of instant gratification can be addictive.

Neuromarketing targets the hyperactivation and constant agitation of the dopamine/endorphin functions of the brain. Addiction directly undermines free will.

Corporations, ranging from the most prestigious firms to pharmaceuticals, to the extraction of raw materials, to air travel and car manufacturing and food production, have a history of wrongdoing, including direct assaults on health. However, even public outrage does not lead to structural change.

A study has found that foods with a high glycemic index get us hungrier faster. They have been seen to activate the same brain regions as stimulated by drugs like cocaine or heroin.

This manipulation has been made possible because of the stresses, disconnections, and dislocations of life that is deep into capitalism. Capitalism brings along with it lifestyle challenges: lack of time, lack of exercise, growing insecurity, lack of family connection, loss of community, and erosion of the social network.

Compulsive overeating is a response to stress. Stress makes people choose unhealthy foods. It also depletes the serotonin/contentment circuits and shifts the brain toward short-term dopamine fueled pleasures.

If we regard corporations as 'persons', many meet the criteria of sociopaths: acting without a conscience, not caring about what happens to others as a consequence of their actions, and not feeling guilt or remorse.

In a country like America, narcissism and sociopathy are not illnesses but strategies. The climate crisis is the best example of the sociopathic behavior of corporate and government spheres.

Goal:

The twenty-first chapter of *The Myth of Normal* discusses how major corporations target the brain circuits of pleasure and reward to foster addictive compulsions. It talks about corporate greed and how capitalism as an ideology breeds stresses, disconnections, and dislocations. We also learn that if corporations are referred to as people, they can be termed as narcissistic and sociopathic.

Lesson:

Activity 1:
In this chapter we learn about how seeking pleasure is a never-ending pursuit. Can you think of rewards that build positive engagement and long-lasting content rather than fleeting highs?

Checklist:

Key learnings from this chapter are:
- [ ] The field called neuromarketing aims to market happiness but what it is actually selling is pleasure.
- [ ] Pleasure and happiness employ different neurochemicals: pleasure works with dopamine and opiates, both of which are short-term; contentment works on serotonin, which is more of a steady and slow release.
- [ ] It is very hard to get addicted to anything serotonin – both substances and behaviors.
- [ ] Addictions control the dopamine (incentive/motivation) and

opiate (pleasure/reward) systems of the brain.
- Neuromarketing targets the hyperactivation and constant agitation of the dopamine/endorphin functions of the brain.
- Capitalism brings along with it lifestyle challenges: lack of time, lack of exercise, growing insecurity, lack of family connection, loss of community, and erosion of the social network.
- If we regard corporations as 'persons', many meet the criteria of sociopaths: acting without a conscience, not caring about what happens to others as a consequence of their actions, and not feeling guilt or remorse.

Action Plan:

- Remember both for yourself and others when you see them displaying this behavior: Compulsive overeating is a response to stress. Stress makes people choose unhealthy foods. It also depletes the serotonin/contentment circuits and shifts the brain toward short-term dopamine fueled pleasures.

Chapter 22: The Assaulted Sense of Self: How Race and Class Get Under the Skin

The twenty-second chapter of *The Myth of Normal* by Gabor Maté and Daniel Maté shares what it feels like to be an "other" in a culture or society.

Self-rejection is powerful. It has physiological dimensions that affect every aspect of well-being. It is racism's sharpest and most intimate harm.

The term *biological embedding* refers to our social environments and experiences shaping our biology and development. Though its impacts are real, race does not exist in physiological or genetic terms. The idea of racism was created because of European capitalism.

Racism is an antidote to self-doubt: if I don't feel good about myself, at least there is someone I can feel superior to. It gives me a sense of power and status.

The Black American psychologist Kenneth Hardy talks about the "assaulted sense of self". It is when one's sense of self is defined by someone else – by what I am not rather than what I am.

Among the many wounds caused by racism are emotional suppression and its biological harms. Overt experiences of racism and the assaulted sense of self accelerate biological aging and shorten life.

Bigotry that is socially entrenched takes an unspoken toll on health. Factors like confinement, deprivation, fear, and suppressed outrage create stress and have a direct impact on the body. Black people in the United States are more likely to suffer from diabetes, obesity, hypertension, and stroke.

The suppression of authenticity interferes with biology and breeds illness. Racial differences defy economic categories, across educational levels and socioeconomic status. The stresses of racial prejudice accrue over time, even in the absence of economic disadvantage. They toxify the body and undermine its capacity to maintain itself.

Stress hormone levels are much higher in children of low economic status. Stressed environments interfere with brain development. A scientist has referred to poverty as a 'neurotoxin'.

Inequality does not affect only the very poor. In a materialist society, a person's relative position on the social ladder is a predictor of health. *Social gradient* is the term used for the link between social rank and health. The lesser control people have, the higher their trigger for physiological stress and illness. Self-image also plays a role. How people judge themselves or our judged by others according to their financial achievement becomes a source of stress that undermines their well-being.

Goal:
The twenty-second chapter of *The Myth of Normal* is a trauma-informed look at race and economic status. Both of these are two major social determinants of health and do not operate as independently. We get to understand how racism, poverty, and inequality create stress that undermines well-being.

Lesson:
Activity 1: Malcolm X urged us to reflect on the following questions. You can use them to confront your own self-loathing: - Who taught you to hate the texture of your hair? - Who taught you to hate the color of your skin to such an extent that you bleach to get the like the white man? - Who taught you to hate the shape of your nose and lips? - Who taught you to hate yourself from the top of your head to the soles of your feet?

Checklist:
Key learnings from this chapter are: ☐ Self-rejection is powerful. It has physiological dimensions that affect every aspect of well-being. ☐ The term *biological embedding* refers to our social environments and experiences shaping our biology and development. ☐ The "assaulted sense of self" is when one's sense of self is defined by someone else – by what I am not rather than what I am. ☐ Overt experiences of racism and the assaulted sense of self accelerate biological aging and shorten life. ☐ The suppression of authenticity interferes with biology and

breeds illness.
- Racial differences defy economic categories, across educational levels and socioeconomic status.
- *Social gradient* is the term used for the link between social rank and health.
- How people judge themselves or our judged by others according to their financial achievement becomes a source of stress that undermines their well-being.

Action Plan:

- Think about the indigenous people in Canada or Black people in America. Do you think they tread the same ground as their Caucasian counterparts, face the same daily obstacles, or navigate the same sorts of adversity?

Chapter 23: Society's Shock Absorbers: Why Women Have It Worse

The twenty-third chapter of *The Myth of Normal* by Gabor Maté and Daniel Maté attempts to address the question – why do women suffer from chronic illnesses far more often than men and why are they far more likely to be diagnosed with mental health conditions?

Gabor says that the gender gap in health is real. Women are more subject to chronic disease and have more years of poor health and disability. The question to ask is: what stresses could women be sharing with Black people as a group? They are both targeted by a culture that demeans, distorts, and impels them to suppress who they are.

In a culture that is sexualized and threatening, many women inevitably develop an "assaulted sense of self".

A healthy response to any kind of assault is anger. It comes from a system of the brain that is intended to defend our boundaries, both physical and emotional. Women's anger tends to be subdued to the detriment of their health. The giving up of the spontaneous "no" is imposed on them more widely and with greater force.

It is different from deliberately holding in anger. Repression occurs without conscious awareness. When we don't even know that we are angry, we cannot resolve or process the problem. Instead, we soothe ourselves with ways like crying or eating.

Self-suppression is reinforced by persistent, gendered social conditioning. Many women learn to self-silence their thoughts and feelings to maintain safe relationships, particularly intimate ones.

A compulsive and self-sacrificing doing for others, suppression of anger, and an excessive concern about social acceptability are features found across all autoimmune diseases. These are the same traits that are inculcated into women in a patriarchal culture.

Sexualization is another source of ill health for women. Pornography influences many boys to associate pleasure with domination and shut their tender feelings.

The task of caring largely falls to women, which is often a stress-inducing, externally imposed role. They serve as the emotional glue, keeping families and communities together. They also suffer far more from diseases of actual connective tissue, such as rheumatoid arthritis and fibromyalgia.

The stress of caregiving weakens the immune system. They also have shorter telomeres, which means premature aging. Men's sense of being entitled to women's care is deeply entrenched in our society. A large part of the disproportionately high rate of anxiety among women comes from their absorption of male angst and the culturally directed responsibility for soothing it.

Men suffer too because of the taboo against vulnerability and the impermissibility of emotions like sadness or grief. Toxified masculinity is lethal. These defenses against or escape from vulnerability, grief, and fear show up as alcoholism and other substance addictions, workaholism, violence, and suicidality.

In our culture, we think boys turn to men through disconnection from their feelings, vulnerabilities, and others. The more vulnerable a man, the more 'girly' he is perceived to be.

Goal:

The twenty-third chapter of *The Myth of Normal* examines the stresses of being a female in a patriarchal society. It attempts to address two questions – why do women suffer from chronic illnesses far more often than men and why are they far more likely to be diagnosed with mental health conditions?

Lesson:

Activity 1:
What are the pressures that you feel because of your gender?

Checklist:

Key learnings from this chapter are:
- Women are more subject to chronic disease and have more years of poor health and disability. They are targeted by a culture that demeans, distorts, and impels them to suppress who they are.
- In a culture that is sexualized and threatening, many women inevitably develop an "assaulted sense of self".
- A healthy response to any kind of assault is anger. Women's anger tends to be subdued to the detriment of their health.
- Many women learn to self-silence their thoughts and feelings to maintain safe relationships, particularly intimate ones.
- A compulsive and self-sacrificing doing for others,

suppression of anger, and an excessive concern about social acceptability are features found across all autoimmune diseases.

☐ Sexualization is another source of ill health for women.

☐ Men suffer too because of the taboo against vulnerability and the impermissibility of emotions like sadness or grief.

Action Plan:

☐ Remember: Suppression leads to disease. The next time you are suppressing an emotion, see if it is possible to find a healthy outlet for its release.

Chapter 24: We Feel Their Pain: Our Trauma-Infused Politics

The twenty-fourth chapter of *The Myth of Normal* by Gabor Maté and Daniel Maté examines the outermost layer of the biopsychosocial onion: the political.

We can confidently say that politics today and the surrounding media culture are more toxic than ever. Political discussion can be so incendiary that conversation is often not even possible. People have reported that politics has resulted in emotional costs and lost friendships. There can be allostatic wear and tear due to politics, resulting in shorter telomeres.

We do not have an escape from politics and headlines because of our phones and social media.

Gabor says the closer he looks at who forms the political landscape, the more he sees the wounded electing the wounded, the traumatized leading the traumatized, and implementing policies embedded in traumatizing social conditions.

Political culture is one of the many avenues through which toxic myths become normalized truths. We expect certain dispositions and worldviews from our leaders. One of them is hardening to vital aspects of emotional life.

The manifestation of trauma on the political stage has massive consequences for people and the planet. Social and environmental maladies like addiction and climate change are alerting us to something amiss in the *body politic*. So are moods of resignation, cynicism, suspicion, and venom.

If we want to understand why individuals and groups believe and behave as they do, we need to see the scars underneath the extreme emotional reactions. We can only do this if we ease our own strong views of rightness and wrongness.

Traumatic childhood experiences directly relate to adult political orientations. The harsher the parenting children experience, the more prone they become to support authoritarian or aggressive policies. All oppressors, without exception, have been seen to go through a strict and rigid upbringing.

People unconsciously look to their leaders to fulfill their own unmet childhood needs. Leaders who exude traits of hostility and authoritarianism can make those of us feel empowered in whom a real sense of power is wanting. In those of us wanting leaders to be kind, supporting, caring, and inclusive, there can be a displaced longing for attuned parenting.

Goal:
The twenty-fourth chapter of *The Myth of Normal* examines the outermost layer of the biopsychosocial onion: the political. We learn about political and celebrity culture and how our leaders are who they are because of their childhood trauma and why we seek who we seek as a leader based on our childhood trauma.

Lesson:
Activity 1: Practice 5 minutes of deep breathing before and after scrolling the news, without exception.

Checklist:
Key learnings from this chapter are: ☐ Politics today and the surrounding media culture are more toxic than ever. ☐ Political discussion can be so incendiary that conversation is often not even possible. ☐ People have reported that politics has resulted in emotional costs and lost friendships. There can be allostatic wear and tear due to politics, resulting in shorter telomeres. ☐ Political culture is one of the many avenues through which toxic myths become normalized truths. ☐ We expect certain dispositions and worldviews from our leaders. One of them is hardening to vital aspects of emotional life. ☐ If we want to understand why individuals and groups believe and behave as they do, we need to see the scars underneath the extreme emotional reactions. ☐ Traumatic childhood experiences directly relate to adult political orientations.

- The harsher the parenting children experience, the more prone they become to support authoritarian or aggressive policies.
- People unconsciously look to their leaders to fulfill their own unmet childhood needs.
- Leaders who exude traits of hostility and authoritarianism can make those of us feel empowered in whom a real sense of power is wanting.
- In those of us wanting leaders to be kind, supporting, caring, and inclusive, there can be a displaced longing for attuned parenting.

Action Plan:

- Would you like to adjust your news consumption habits to better filter out the rancor, anxiety, spite, and doom?
- Is it possible to practice better listening and exercise more empathy with those with whom we disagree?

Chapter 25: Mind in the Lead: The Possibility of Healing

The twenty-fifth chapter of *The Myth of Normal* by Gabor Maté and Daniel Maté delves into the topic of healing.

Healing is a natural movement toward wholeness. Gabor says healing is a direction, not a destination. It is not synonymous with self-development but is closer to self-retrieval. It is engaging in recovering lost parts of the self, not trying to change or improve them. It is also different from being cured, which is the absence of disease.

Gabor says it is possible to be abstinent without being sober. Abstinence is the avoidance or absence of something. Sobriety is the capacity to be in the present and experience life as it is.

We do not need healing in order to be cured. It is an end in itself.

The journey toward healing begins with an acknowledgment of our suffering and the suffering of others. It means opening ourselves to the truth of our past and present, plainly and objectively. An honest assessment can be very hard because the truth hurts and our illusions cover our discomfort.

Healing brings the heart and mind into alignment and cooperation. If the heart is the compass to the path of healing, the mind is the territory to be navigated.

We construct the world that we live in with our minds. Modern psychology, however, shows us how the world creates our minds before our minds can create the world. The way out is that we remain the ones creating the world we see in every moment.

Moving forward, we can learn to be responsible for the mind with which we create our world. The capacity to heal needs the willingness to take responsibility. It is a moment-by-moment commitment.

Our mental prison is built and fenced by the meaning we give to events not just by the events themselves. Gabor speaks of his conviction that within everyone there is the potential for growth and development, no matter what their experiences, beliefs, or actions.

Gabor also shares how he was advised to let go of the past, not clutching to its pain and resentment, nor to the beliefs he developed at a time he could not have known any better. He says this is a freedom worth seeking.

Goal:

The twenty-fifth chapter of *The Myth of Normal* delves into the topic of healing. It points to the possibility of healing on individual and societal levels in a culture that is increasingly anxious and disordered. Gabor offers suggestions on what healing asks of us and the inner and outer conditions that are most conducive to its flourishing.

Lesson:

Activity 1:
We learn about true healing. Open yourself to the truth of your life. Make a plain and objective assessment of your past and present. Acknowledge where you are wounded and perform an honest audit of the impact of those wounds both on yourself and others around you.

Checklist:

Key learnings from this chapter are:
- [ ] Healing is a natural movement toward wholeness.
- [ ] It is engaging in recovering lost parts of the self, not trying to change or improve them.
- [ ] It is also different from being cured, which is the absence of disease.

- Abstinence is the avoidance or absence of something. Sobriety is the capacity to be in the present and experience life as it is.
- We do not need healing in order to be cured. It is an end in itself.
- The journey toward healing begins with an acknowledgment of our suffering and the suffering of others.
- If the heart is the compass to the path of healing, the mind is the territory to be navigated.
- Moving forward, we can learn to be responsible for the mind with which we create our world.
- Our mental prison is built and fenced by the meaning we give to events not just by the events themselves.

Action Plan:

- Ask yourself if you are ready to be on the healing path – not needing to be perfect or exercising saintly compassion or reaching any emotional or spiritual benchmark, but just the readiness to participate in whatever process wants to unfold within you so that healing can happen naturally.

Chapter 26: Four A's and Five Compassions: Some Healing Principles

The twenty-sixth chapter of *The Myth of Normal* by Gabor Maté and Daniel Maté begins by saying that the path of healing is deeply personal.

No one can plot someone else's course of healing. However, we can sketch out the territory, describe it, familiarize ourselves with it, and prepare to meet its challenges. We can also learn about the natural laws of healing and the attitudes and attributes it awakens and responds to within us. It cannot be mandated or hastened but facilitated.

The following four A's are healing principles and represent a healthy quality corresponding to a human need.

1. Authenticity: It is difficult to capture the full essence of this word. Words like genuineness, truthfulness, and originality are often used. Authenticity is something lived and experienced. It cannot be pursued, only embodied.

We can help ourselves by noticing when authenticity is not there and then using curiosity and gentle skepticism to the limiting self-beliefs that stand in its way.

When we can admit to ourselves that we are scared or we didn't mean what we said or that hurt, it is our impulse toward authenticity becoming stronger. We are now able to catch ourselves and it is then that new choices emerge.

2. Agency: It is the capacity to freely take responsibility for our existence and exercise response ability in all decisions that affect us. Not having agency is a source of stress. It could arise from social or political conditions or illness.

Exercising agency is powerfully healing.

3. Anger: Anger is not blind rage, resentment, spite, venom, or bile, which come from unexpressed or unintegrated emotions. Suppressed and amplified out of proportion anger are both toxic.

Healthy anger is a natural boundary defense that gets activated when we perceive a threat to our physical or emotional integrity. It is a response of the moment, situational, and of limited duration. It does its job of fending off the threat and then subsides. Anger does not have moral content of right or wrong and does not intend anyone any harm. Its only desire is to maintain integrity and equilibrium.

Many of us learn to minimize our anger. Some of us don't even know what it looks like. The task for us is to check ourselves when we find ourselves tolerating or explaining away situations that stress us. We can practice giving anger some space to come up.

Anger expression can support physical health.

4. Acceptance: It is allowing things to be as they are, however they are. It is not complacency or resignation, rejecting or condoning. It is the recognition that in this moment, things cannot be other than how they are. We just be with the truth and create a relationship with the actual, present moment. Acceptance also demands that we face that we don't know how we feel or that our feelings are mixed.

There is a difference between accepting and tolerating. One is being with something; the other is putting up with something. Acceptance makes room for anger, agency, and authenticity. Tolerating, on the other hand, involves rejecting one's needs, values, and integrity.

The Five Compassions

Gabor says he has distinguished five levels of compassion that build on and reinforce one another non-hierarchically. They can encourage, guide, and orient us toward the path of wholeness.

1. Ordinary Human Compassion: It is the ability to be with suffering and being moved by the awareness that someone is struggling. It necessarily involves empathy and can be worn down or depleted but bounces back once we can get the rest and replenishment we need.

Empathy serves as our mirror by showing us our own emotional-injury history if we observe in what situations and toward whom we harden our hearts and shut down.

2. The Compassion of Curiosity and Understanding: It believes that everything exists for a reason and the reason matters. It is the compassion of context – asking ourselves why someone would end up being the way they are and act the way they do.

3. The Compassion of Recognition: It allows us to perceive and appreciate that we are all in this together, experiencing similar tribulations and contradictions. In the absence of recognizing our commonality, we can get caught up in the stress of judgment and resistance.

We can inquire into our judging mind with compassionate curiosity.

125

4. The Compassion of Truth: The mission to shield people from life's inevitable hurts, disappointments, and setbacks can be counterproductive and even inauthentic. They come from our discomfort with our own woundedness.

This principle recognizes that pain is not the enemy. Instead, it alerts us to what is amiss.

5. The Compassion of Possibility: It is understanding that there is more to each of us than what we present to the world and the behaviors that we act out. It is connected to wonder, awe, mystery, and imagination. It recognizes that we can actualize, at any moment, whatever we need and long for.

Goal:

The twenty-sixth chapter of *The Myth of Normal* takes us further into healing. No one can plot someone else's course of healing. However, we can sketch out the territory, describe it, familiarize ourselves with it, and prepare to meet its challenges. We can also learn about the natural laws of healing and the attitudes and attributes it awakens and responds to within us.

Lesson:

Activity 1:
When authenticity is lacking, there is tension or anxiety, irritability or regret, depression or fatigue. When any of these surfaces, ask yourself:
Is there an inner guidance I am defying, resisting, ignoring, or avoiding?
Are there truths I am not expressing or even contemplating because of my fear of losing security or belonging?
When I interact with others, is there some way I have abandoned myself, my needs, my values?
What fears, rationalizations, or familiar narratives kept me from being myself?
Do I even know what my own values are?

Checklist:

Key learnings from this chapter are:
- [ ] Authenticity is something lived and experienced. It cannot be pursued, only embodied.
- [ ] Agency is the capacity to freely take responsibility for our existence and exercise response ability in all decisions that affect us.
- [ ] Healthy anger is a natural boundary defense that gets

activated when we perceive a threat to our physical or emotional integrity.

☐ Acceptance is allowing things to be as they are, however they are.

☐ Ordinary Human Compassion is the ability to be with suffering and being moved by the awareness that someone is struggling.

☐ The Compassion of Curiosity and Understanding believes that everything exists for a reason and the reason matters.

☐ The Compassion of Recognition allows us to perceive and appreciate that we are all in this together, experiencing similar tribulations and contradictions.

☐ The Compassion of Truth recognizes that pain is not the enemy. Instead, it alerts us to what is amiss.

☐ The Compassion of Possibility is understanding that there is more to each of us than what we present to the world and the behaviors that we act out.

Action Plan:

☐ Remember the 4 A's and the 5 Compassions:
A's: Authenticity, Agency, Anger, Acceptance
Compassions: Ordinary Human Compassion, The Compassion of Curiosity and Understanding, The Compassion of Recognition, The Compassion of Truth, The Compassion of Possibility

Chapter 27: A Dreadful Gift: Disease as Teacher

The twenty-seventh chapter of *The Myth of Normal* by Gabor Maté and Daniel Maté talks about how we can find value and meaning in illness. Some people even go as far as to call their disease a cherished gift.

It is possible for us to heal through disease rather than merely healing from it. Also, Gabor says, that what we are exploring is getting whole and not getting better. The blessing that people talk about is that of healing and not of cure. While cure is never guaranteed, healing is available to us until our last breath.

Gabor shares a story of how a lady with rheumatoid arthritis engaged in compassionate inquiry toward herself and experienced self-transformation. There ensued an increase in awareness, equanimity, joy, health, and satisfaction.

The body is calling us back to an integration of the Self, all of the independent parts, including the ones that are exiled and the ones that are protectors, through emotional or physical indicators.

Gabor says it is possible for all of us to find healing by gaining the capacity to accept life as it really is, using authenticity to search for our own truth in all situations, and having the agency to choose our response to whatever occurs.

Psychiatrist Dr. Jeffrey Rediger, who has studied many cases of miraculous recovery from fatal diseases, says a transformation of identity is the key. That is where healing is to be found. These people change their beliefs about themselves and the world.

A brain cancer survivor spoke about how his disease brought the truth of his mortality into a more real, felt dimension. It created for him an extraordinary degree of shared presence, listening, and care. Total transformation.

Healing necessarily involves the complete and whole-hearted acceptance of our mortality.

Goal:

The twenty-seventh chapter of *The Myth of Normal* shares with us true stories of people who have recovered from fatal diseases through their journey of complete self-transformation. The authors talk about how we can find value and meaning in illness. Some people even go as far as to call their disease a cherished gift.

Lesson:

Activity 1:
If you have any kind of physical discomfort or disease, focus on the symptom and get curious about it. Ask questions of it. You might encounter the part that is using the symptom to get a message through and try and express itself. Listen to what it has to say.

Checklist:

Key learnings from this chapter are:
- [ ] It is possible for us to heal through disease rather than merely healing from it.
- [ ] The blessing that people talk about is that of healing and not of cure. While cure is never guaranteed, healing is available to us until our last breath.

- The body is calling us back to an integration of the Self, all of the independent parts, including the ones that are exiled and the ones that are protectors, through emotional or physical indicators.
- It is possible for all of us to find healing by gaining the capacity to accept life as it really is, using authenticity to search for our own truth in all situations, and having the agency to choose our response to whatever occurs.
- Psychiatrist Dr. Jeffrey Rediger, who has studied many cases of miraculous recovery from fatal diseases, says a transformation of identity is the key.
- Healing necessarily involves the complete and whole-hearted acceptance of our mortality.

Action Plan:

- Reflect on your mortality. Can you feel joy in being alive and wake up every morning with full-hearted acceptance of this truth so you can make the most of this life?

Chapter 28: Before the Body Says No: First Steps on the Return to Self

The twenty-eighth chapter of *The Myth of Normal* by Gabor Maté and Daniel Maté offers simple but potent practices, distilled from Gabor's work with thousands of people that can retrain body and mind to become more sensitive and responsive to the subtle alerts that our lives unfailingly send our way.

While doing these exercises, it may be helpful to keep these principles in mind:

a) Your personality is not you; you are not your personality.

b) The personality is an adaptation: Our personality is mostly a jumble of genuine traits and conditioned coping styles. Some of these do not reflect our true self. Healing asks us to free ourselves from this automatic programming.

c) Our bodies do keep the score: We can heed the messages the body sends us by learning its language.

d) The personality, and the loss of our essential nature, is not personal: The disconnect from self is rooted in our materialist culture.

Gabor shares with us the practice he has developed: Compassionate Inquiry (CI). He says an inquiry is an open-ended exploration that needs humility. It also needs a suspension of whatever we believe we know about ourselves. It is an attempt to know ourselves, not about ourselves.

The second piece compassion needs openness, patience, and generosity. Think of someone you love and the leeway you would give their confusion, perplexity, or frustration. We need to give ourselves the same. It is an invitation to inquire into the what, why, and how of our limiting beliefs and behaviors. It is practiced with complete non-judgment.

A Self-Inquiry Exercise:

This is to be done daily or weekly and needs commitment over time. It is best done in a written form, in a quiet room free of distractions. Writing by hand helps to create a connection with yourself. It is to be done minimum once a week.

Question 1: In my life's important areas, what am I not saying no to? Where did I, sense a "no" within me that wanted to be expressed, but I stifled it, saying a yes where a no wanted to be heard?

Question 2: How does my inability to say no impact my life? This impact lands itself in three main spheres:

- the physical – bodily warning signs like insomnia, back pain, muscle spasms, dry mouth, frequent colds, abdominal pains, digestive problems, fatigue, headaches, skin rashes, loss of appetite, and the urge to overeat
- the emotional – shows up as sadness, alienation, anxiety, or boredom. Can also manifest as emotional deficits.
- the interpersonal – resentment towards the people or situations where the authentic answer was stifled

Question 3: What bodily signals have I been overlooking? What symptoms have I been ignoring that could be warning signs, were I to pay conscious attention?

Question 4: What is the hidden story behind my inability to say no? This entails identifying the narrative, the explanation, the justification, the rationalization that makes our habits seem normal and even necessary.

Question 5: Where did I learn these stories? The intention is to look at the past but rather than dwelling on it, letting it go.

Question 6: Where have I ignored or denied the "yes" that wanted to be said? Withholding an authentic yes can also make us ill. What have you wanted to do, manifest, create, or say that you have forsaken in the name of duty or out of fear?

Goal:
The twenty-eighth chapter of *The Myth of Normal* offers simple but potent practices, distilled from Gabor's work with thousands of people that can retrain body and mind to become more sensitive and responsive to the subtle alerts that our lives unfailingly send our way.

Lesson:
Activity 1: Create a journal and start a daily/weekly answering of the 6 questions that Gabor gives us in his process of Compassionate Inquiry.

Checklist:
Key learnings from this chapter are: ☐ An inquiry is an open-ended exploration that needs humility. ☐ It also needs a suspension of whatever we believe we know about ourselves. ☐ It is an attempt to know ourselves, not about ourselves. ☐ The second piece compassion needs openness, patience, and generosity. ☐ Think of someone you love and the leeway you would give their confusion, perplexity, or frustration. We need to give ourselves the same. ☐ It is an invitation to inquire into the what, why, and how of our limiting beliefs and behaviors. It is practiced with complete non-judgment.

Action Plan:

- [ ] Remember the 4 principles:
    a) Your personality is not you; you are not your personality.

    b) The personality is an adaptation.

    c) Our bodies do keep the score.

    d) The personality, and the loss of our essential nature, is not personal.

Chapter 29: Seeing is Disbelieving: Undoing Self-Limiting Beliefs

The twenty-ninth chapter of *The Myth of Normal* by Gabor Maté and Daniel Maté shares with us the most self-limiting story: I am not worth it. If unaddressed, it sabotages all of our efforts to practice compassionate inquiry.

This conviction of unworthiness is deeply entrenched within us. We should not underestimate how insidious it is or how difficult it is to throw it out with words.

The following exercise suggests some steps. The method is experiential and requires commitment and mindfulness. It is effective when practiced regularly and also when a self-undermining belief shows up. Choose a quiet place to sit and write, preferably in a handwritten journal.

Step 1: Relabel

Identify the self-limiting thought as a thought or a belief, not the truth. Bringing conscious awareness is vital. It helps us awaken to the part in us that can observe mental content without identifying with it. You are not trying to debunk the story or prove that it is wrong. Nor are you trying to replace it with a cheerful opposite.

Step 2: Reattribute

You learn to assign the relabeled belief to its proper source. You are not blaming yourself or anyone else. But you ascribe the cause to its proper place. You are not pushing. You are making clear that you did not ask for it nor have you deserved it.

Step 3: Refocus

Buy yourself some time. The negative self-beliefs will pass if you give them time. If you manage to catch a negative self-belief that is trying to take control, find something else to do. Take about 15 minutes and choose something that you enjoy and will keep you active, preferably something healthy and creative.

The purpose is to teach the brain that it does not have to give in to the old story. It can learn to do something else, if only for a short while.

Step 4: Revalue

Ask yourself the question: What has this belief actually done for me? Allow your answers to go beyond the conceptual.

Step 5: Recreate

Ask yourself what has determined your identity up until now. It is time to recreate and imagine a different life. Write down your values and intentions.

Goal:

The twenty-ninth chapter of *The Myth of Normal* shares with us the most self-limiting story: I am not worth it. If unaddressed, it sabotages all of our efforts to practice compassionate inquiry. Gabor gives us 5 steps to overcome this.

Lesson:

Activity 1:
Create a journal and start a daily/weekly practice of writing down your answers to the 5 steps shared by Gabor for overcoming limiting self-beliefs.

Checklist:

Key learnings from this chapter are:
- [ ] The conviction of unworthiness is deeply entrenched within us.
- [ ] We should not underestimate how insidious it is or how difficult it is to throw it out with words.
- [ ] Bringing conscious awareness to our limiting beliefs helps us awaken to the part in us that can observe mental content without identifying with it.
- [ ] The negative self-beliefs will pass if you give them time.
- [ ] It is possible to teach the brain that it does not have to give in to the old story. It can learn to do something else, if only for a short while.

Action Plan:

- [ ] Think about an activity that you enjoy doing; something that is healthy and creative, that you can use to re-focus in Step 3 of Gabor's model.

Chapter 30: Foes to Friends: Working with the Obstacles to Healing

The thirtieth chapter of *The Myth of Normal* by Gabor Maté and Daniel Maté offers a way of working with some of the most universal obstacles to healing: crippling guilt; self-loathing and its close cousins - self-rejection, self-sabotage, and self-destructive impulses; and blocks in our emotional memory, which is essentially denial of pain.

Everything within us is there for a purpose. There is nothing there that should not be. We need to shift the narrative from "How do I get rid of this?" to "What is this for? Why is it here?"

When we turn these foes into friends we realize that their origins were protective and that still remains their objective. They have always been friends. They do not need to be feared, rejected, avoided, or suppressed.

One such friend is chronic guilt. We can think of it as harm reduction. When an adult requires a child to suppress parts of her true self, she needs to develop an enforcement mechanism to prevent disappointing or being cut off from the caregiver. Guilt is the most reliable invigilator.

We can recognize guilt for what it is and make room for it. And we can then consciously decide whether we need to act based on it or not.

Then there is self-accusation. Gabor usually asks some questions to a person when this comes up: If this were a trial and you were the defendant, what would the prosecution have to say about you? What is the verdict here? Because you have done all of these things, that makes you what? What about the sense of feeling all these negative things you feel about yourself? How familiar is that? And how far does it go back?

This belief too has a protective function. When things fall apart for a child, they can either feel that they are unsafe or that they are flawed. Believing that the deficiency is ours gives us a sense of agency and hope. Maybe if we work hard enough, we can earn the love and care we need.

Allowing the self-loathing to exist relaxes its totalitarian hold.

Then there are compensatory afflictions like addictions and mental illness. These are dynamic processes and not solid things and can be turned into allies.

Mental and personality disorders can have helpful dimensions too.

For those of us who cannot remember much of our childhoods, it is good to remember that we do not require the past, only the present. We can always work with the here and now. Also, it is not true that we do not remember. Our memories show up in our relationship to ourselves and others.

Goal:

The thirtieth chapter of *The Myth of Normal* offers a way of working with some of the most universal obstacles to healing: crippling guilt; self-loathing and its close cousins - self-rejection, self-sabotage, and self-destructive impulses; and blocks in our emotional memory, which is denial of pain.

Lesson:

Activity 1:
If you have a conscious recall of a happy childhood and yet you are confronting chronic illness, emotional distress, addiction, or struggles to be authentic, ask yourself:
When I felt sad, unhappy, angry, confused, bewildered, lonely, or bullied, as a child who did I speak to? Who did I tell? Who could I confide in?

Checklist:

Key learnings from this chapter are:
- [ ] We need to shift the narrative from "How do I get rid of this?" to "What is this for? Why is it here?"
- [ ] When we turn these foes into friends we realize that their origins were protective and that still remains their objective.
- [ ] One such friend is chronic guilt. We can think of it as harm reduction.

- When things fall apart for a child, they can either feel that they are unsafe or that they are flawed. Believing that the deficiency is ours gives us a sense of agency and hope.
- For those of us who cannot remember much of our childhoods, it is good to remember that we do not require the past, only the present. We can always work with the here and now.
- Also, it is not true that we do not remember. Our memories show up in our relationship to ourselves and others.

Action Plan:

- What are your negative self-beliefs? Can you use the process provided by Gabor to identify them and attribute them to where they belong?

Chapter 31: Jesus in the Tipi: Psychedelics and Healing

The thirty-first chapter of *The Myth of Normal* by Gabor Maté and Daniel Maté shares with us Gabor's story of his visit to The Temple of the Way of Light, where shamanic retreats take place.

In these events led by Gabor, there is a combination of the Amazonian tradition of *vegetalismo*, an ancient and highly sophisticated system of plant healing, with his Compassionate Inquiry therapeutic approach.

The shamans conduct the plant sessions at night. Gabor works earlier in the day, helping people formulate their intentions for the ceremony. The following day he helps them process and integrate whatever came up for them.

Gabor then describes how the ceremony takes place. While most participants experience some form of catharsis, Gabor steels himself and predictably, nothing happens. He is almost dissociated and tells himself that it is not about him.

After lunch, the shamans tell Gabor that they would not like him to be around because his energy was dark and dense and interfered in their work with the other participants. For the next ten days, Gabor was socially isolated while every night a shaman would pour him a medicine and chant to him for more than three hours. On the last day, Gabor finally found a release and had a vision of the word happy in Hungarian.

Gabor says that over the years, he has developed reverence for the synergistic power of psychedelics. He has seen people find liberation from ingrained, habitual, and constrictive patterns.

He says the therapeutic use of psychedelics needs a proper setting and the right intention and guidance. They can then help process pain and sorrow and develop peace, love, and joy.

Many have also found psychedelics to be transformational teachers. It is believed that each plant has its own wisdom to impart that can take years of dedicated practice to absorb.

Psychedelics can exert such potent transformative effects because of the mind-body unity and through their power to access the unconscious where many of our emotions and motivations reside. They open up the membrane between the conscious and unconscious mind. They can help facilitate a renewed relationship with the self and the world.

Goal:

The thirty-first chapter of *The Myth of Normal* shares with us Gabor's story of his visit to The Temple of the Way of Light, where shamanic retreats take place. It also talks about the merits of psychedelics and what they can do for us.

Lesson:

Activity 1:
In this chapter, Gabor talks about his resistance to self-healing when going through the shamanic process. Think about ways in which you could be resisting your healing.

Checklist:

Key learnings from this chapter are:
- [ ] In the shamanic events led by Gabor, there is a combination of the Amazonian tradition of *vegetalismo*, an ancient and highly sophisticated system of plant healing, with his Compassionate Inquiry therapeutic approach.
- [ ] Gabor says that over the years, he has developed reverence for the synergistic power of psychedelics.
- [ ] He has seen people find liberation from ingrained, habitual, and constrictive patterns.
- [ ] The therapeutic use of psychedelics needs a proper setting and the right intention and guidance.
- [ ] They can then help process pain and sorrow and develop peace, love, and joy.
- [ ] It is believed that each plant has its own wisdom to impart

that can take years of dedicated practice to absorb.
- [ ] Psychedelics can exert such potent transformative effects because of the mind-body unity and through their power to access the unconscious where many of our emotions and motivations reside.
- [ ] They open up the membrane between the conscious and unconscious mind.
- [ ] They can help facilitate a renewed relationship with the self and the world.

Action Plan:

- [ ] If you are interested to learn more about psychedelics, Gabor mentions the book How to *Change Your Mind: What the New Science of Psychedelics Teaches Us About Consciousness, Dying, Addiction, Depression, and Transcendence* by Michael Pollan.

Chapter 32: My Life as a Genuine Thing: Touching Spirit

The thirty-second chapter of *The Myth of Normal* by Gabor Maté and Daniel Maté begins with Gabor talking about how, until his experience with psychedelics, spirituality had existed for him only second-hand. His faith in a person's genuine transformation, while sincere, was never directly experienced.

What Gabor learned in Peru went beyond belief and spoke to the essence of healing. He became aware of himself as an expanse of consciousness. The experience unfastened his unbelief.

The first thing he learned was that healing is outside the thinking mind's box. The second thing he learned was that he could not have planned this. The third thing was that he had to give up his identity as leader or healer, put aside his habit of helping others without focusing on his own transformation, and see past the protests of his threatened ego.

He was put in a position where he had no control. His only choice was to let go and trust. The letting go was a prerequisite to healing.

While not everyone will work with shamans, the universal healing principles remain the same: acceptance, shedding of identity, choosing to trust our inner guidance, and a genuine agency that arises from the willingness to give up rigid control.

It also taught Gabor what healing is not. It does not have to be a monumental catharsis. It is not the past that has to change, only our present relationship to ourselves.

He says there is more to being human than meets the eye. We are all part of something greater than the ego mind.

One of the most challenging aspects of recovery is to entrust one's life to the care of a higher power. Whether we know it or not, we are all seeking our higher power. It manifests in our desire to belong, our drive to know our purpose, the urge to escape the limitations of our personalities, and our inclination toward transcendent experiences.

Spirituality defies both prescription and description. There are countless routes. Some appeal more than others to different people. Any activity that brings us back to our own nature can be a fountain of refreshment.

Oneness with Nature has been a pillar of the world's indigenous peoples since forever. For them, they have a commitment to Earth and a role in helping Her and the rest of life to thrive. These traditions can provide us with ways to honor our social, emotional, communal, and spiritual needs. Here, healing is a spiritual journey.

To find your own special truth, you need to listen patiently to yourself and give yourself a chance to find your own unique way.

Goal:

The thirty-second chapter of *The Myth of Normal* begins with Gabor talking about how, until his experience with psychedelics, spirituality had existed for him only second-hand. His faith in a person's genuine transformation, while sincere, was never directly experienced. We also learn about the universal healing principles and how the world's indigenous peoples look at healing.

Lesson:

Activity 1:
We learn about the many benefits of developing a mindfulness practice. Try and sit every day for some time while observing yourself with compassionate curiosity rather than judgment. It can also help you drop your prejudices against others.

Checklist:

Key learnings from this chapter are:
- While not everyone will work with shamans, the universal healing principles remain the same: acceptance, shedding of identity, choosing to trust our inner guidance, and a genuine agency that arises from the willingness to give up rigid control.
- Healing does not have to be a monumental catharsis.
- It is not the past that has to change, only our present relationship to ourselves.
- We are all part of something greater than the ego mind.
- Whether we know it or not, we are all seeking our higher power. It manifests in our desire to belong, our drive to know our purpose, the urge to escape the limitations of our personalities, and our inclination toward transcendent

experiences.
- Any activity that brings us back to our own nature can be a fountain of refreshment.
- Oneness with Nature has been a pillar of the world's indigenous peoples since forever.
- These traditions can provide us with ways to honor our social, emotional, communal, and spiritual needs.
- To find your own special truth, you need to listen patiently to yourself and give yourself a chance to find your own unique way.

Action Plan:

- Think about all the metaphors that you can give to the natural world. For example, mountains as symbols of strength and constancy; Rivers embody change and flow.

Chapter 33: Unmaking a Myth: Visioning a Saner Society

The thirty-third chapter of *The Myth of Normal* by Gabor Maté and Daniel Maté begins with the question: What will it take to unmake the myth of normal?

Gabor says he feels a sense of responsibility to offer some sort of alternative vision to the toxic culture he has been depicting. He says for society to right itself, certain conditions will have to be met. The key shifts are derived from the core principles of this book: biopsychosocial medicine, disease as teacher, the foremost importance of both attachment and authenticity, and fearless self-inquiry.

We need to approach this daunting task from a place of possibility. It necessarily involves patience and perspective, and a healthy tolerance for the real as well as the ideal. We must be eager to shed our illusions.

Ignorance can create a seemingly blissful tranquillity but it is not true bliss. On the collective level, it can cause great and wide suffering. We do ourselves and the world a huge favor when we try and dissolve our illusions and open ourselves to the truths they hide. Nothing can be changed until it is faced.

The process demands confronting denial. Each of us is tasked with seeking out and supporting alternative sources of knowledge, exposing ourselves to uncertainty, and entering into the points of view of others. This would create a new kind of citizenship that arises from the needs and demands of the moment.

We need to create a trauma-literate society. There has been a sea change in the public's recognition of trauma's prevalence and significance. Here are the different elements of a trauma-conscious society:

Trauma Awareness: Medicine

A trauma-informed medical system could help heal and prevent suffering on a scale. There needs to be empathy training for medical staff and doctors. There needs to be education about the mind-body unity and the link between adversity and disease.

Trauma Awareness: The Law

A trauma-informed legal system would dedicate itself to correcting things in a humane way. While it would not justify or excuse harmful behavior, programs would be designed to rehabilitate people and not further traumatize them.

Trauma Awareness: Education

A trauma-informed education system would train teachers to be educated about the science of development. It would encourage an atmosphere where emotional intelligence is valued. It would provide a setting where all children were encouraged to thrive.

There are two more A's that we need for broad transformational change: activism and advocacy. Some added ingredients are solidarity, collective thinking, and connection. We need these to counter capitalism and its effects.

The antidote to the influence of normality is authenticity. It is finding meaning in one's inner experience that is unobscured by society's version of what should be. Falsehood is the ultimate abnormality.

All we need to do is to wake up.

Goal:
The thirty-third chapter of *The Myth of Normal* begins with the question: What will it take to unmake the myth of normal? Gabor says he feels a sense of responsibility to offer some sort of alternative vision to the toxic culture he has been depicting. The key shifts are derived from the core principles of this book: biopsychosocial medicine, disease as teacher, the foremost importance of both attachment and authenticity, and fearless self-inquiry.

Lesson:
Activity 1: Try and answer Gabor's questions: Would you prefer to be illusioned or disillusioned?   Would you rather engage with the world as it really is or only as you wish it were?   Which approach brings more suffering in the end?

Checklist:

Key learnings from this chapter are:
- ☐ Ignorance can create a seemingly blissful tranquillity but it is not true bliss. On the collective level, it can cause great and wide suffering.
- ☐ Nothing can be changed until it is faced.
- ☐ Each of us is tasked with seeking out and supporting alternative sources of knowledge, exposing ourselves to uncertainty, and entering into the points of view of others.
- ☐ We need to create a trauma-literate society.
- ☐ A trauma-informed medical system could help heal and prevent suffering on a scale.
- ☐ A trauma-informed legal system would dedicate itself to correcting things in a humane way.
- ☐ A trauma-informed education system would train teachers to be educated about the science of development.
- ☐ There are two more A's that we need for broad transformational change: activism and advocacy.
- ☐ The antidote to the influence of normality is authenticity.

Action Plan:

- ☐ Imagine what our world would look like if we placed young people's well-being at the forefront. What would it mean for parenting and for support for parenting? What would it mean for childcare and education, for the economy, for what products we sell and buy, and for what foods we sell and prepare?
- ☐ Can we raise children who are in touch with their feelings, authentically empowered to express them and to think independently, and be prepared to act on behalf of their principles?

Thank You!

Hope you've enjoyed your reading experience.

We here at Ingenious Reads will always strive to deliver to you the highest quality guides.

So, I'd like to thank you for supporting us and reading until the very end.

Before you go, would you mind leaving us a review on Amazon?

It will mean a lot to us and support us in creating high-quality guides for you in the future.

Warmly yours,

The **Ingenious Reads** Team

Made in the USA
Las Vegas, NV
07 January 2024

84056419R00089